"Bobbi McKenna is a unique original who will WOW you!"

— Mark Victor Hansen,
NY Times # 1 Best Selling author of Chicken Soup for the Soul.

"Telling Your Story is a wonderful GIFT for yourself, your friends, and members of your family that will have lasting meaning for everyone you love!"

— Monique Gavazzi, President of The Foundation for Greater Living, and author of an upcoming humor book for women, Pittsburgh, Pa.

"Telling Your Story is a tool that will enrich and transform your life!"

— Rita Emmett, TODAY SHOW Guest, and Best Selling Author of the Procrastinator's Handbook and The Procrastinating Child.

"Bobbi McKenna's Write Your Own Book Club has shown me how to download the book that has been stuck in my brain." —
Donna Barrett Gilbert, EMMY AWARD WINNER, and author of Hair Power, Malibu, California.

"There are so many people out there, taking advantage of aspiring writers. Bobbi McKenna's Write Your Own Book Club is the real deal! She comes through with the goods: solid information you can use. In less than a month, my book is well on its way to completion."

— Lynley Summers, author of
Autism Is Not A Life Sentence! Jacksonville, Arkansas.

"Bobbi McKenna is a human dynamo, brimming with wisdom, new ideas, energy, and creativity. She helped me focus my media initiatives. I highly recommend Bobbi to any person who wants to move into the big leagues."

— Angelo Paparelli, Attorney At Law,
Immigration Expert and author, Irvine, California.

"Joining The Write Your own Book Club™ has been one of the best decisions I've ever made. It's a well-organized, comprehensive, and flexible approach to writing a book that anyone can follow. Bobbi McKenna is a wonderful mentor who has changed the way I view myself and helped me realize my dream of authorship. Thank you, Bobbi!"

— Rachel Foster, President of Planning Matters, and author of
Biznastics™ How To Power Up Your Business in Thirty Days!
Edmonton, Alberta, Canada.

"Being part of Bobbi McKenna's Write Your Own Book Club™ is helping me transform the teleclass I've been teaching for two years into a published book and a guided meditation CD far more easily than I'd imagined was possible. Bobbi believes that everyone has a story to share. Her support, experience, and tips have been invaluable in making this come true for me and my book!"

— Barbara Schiffman, Life Balance Coach,
and author of Quantum Shift Your Life! Los Angeles, California.

"As a personal coach and author, I appreciate the benefits of coaching in a busy world. Talking about a book idea and actually disciplining one's self to write it are worlds apart. Bobbi's weekly Book Club teleconferences provide structure, marketing tips, and encouragement absent in a writer's isolated world."

— Sally Landau, Life Coach and co-author of COLLEGE SHOCK,
How To Survive the First Year of College, Los Angeles, California.

Telling Your Story

~

Why it's important, and how to do it the easy way!

By

Bobbi McKenna

"Telling Your Story" is a Trademark Owned by Bobbi McKenna

Total Success Solutions Publishing
Centennial, Colorado

Published by:
Total Success Solutions Publishing
Centennial, Colorado

Copyright © 2004 Bobbi McKenna
ISBN, print ed. 0-9727360-4-2

Library of Congress Control Number: 2003099125
Printed in the United States of America

This book is dedicated to

My husband Robert,

And to my family,

past, present, and future!

Table of Contents

Acknowledgements

Thanks to Valerie Allen, John Alston, John Blanchette, Lori Eaton, Vern Eaton, Rita Emmett, George Foster, Rachel Foster, Monique Gavazzi, Donna Gilbert, Sally Landau, Sue Leonard, Christopher McKenna, Hilary McKenna, Jason McKenna, Spencer McKenna, Susan Richards, Barbara Schiffman, Chris Smith, and Lynley Summers.

License

Introduction

"Fiords, Sailing Ships, and Seeing All The Way To America"

Each of our lives forms a powerful and compelling story whether we are aware of it or not. What makes us unique and irreplaceable is shaped and known through the little details of our lives. The places we live, the people we love, and the way we spend our time — all of these influence the choices we make, and in the end, it is the choices we make that define who we are.

Some of our stories will be remembered and repeated. Some will even serve as models of inspiration for others as they seek to build their own strong connections with the world around them. Only a few life stories will endure while most will be forgotten — not because the first group of stories are more worthy — but simply because they were written down.

I know about the talents, hopes, dreams, joys, and fears of my father's family in Norway because of one woman. Her name was Thora Franklin, and she was my grandfather's sister. At the age of seventy-two, Flora sat down and wrote her own story.

What she wrote covers a mere four pages, but those four pages convey more of the spirit of real living people than many long family histories that detail one dry fact after another.

What was it that moved Thora Franklin to write her story? I'll never know for sure. What I do know is that she recorded details that have meaning to me.

Because of what she wrote, I know that my Great Grandfather was a violinist and a violinmaker. I know that the Franklin Family lived in a beautiful valley called "Saterdalen" on an estate called "Loiland." I know that they rowed a boat across a creek to go to church, and that the children went to school on skis.

Whether the place names are correct, or not, isn't as important to me as the images Thora paints with her words. In my mind's eye, I can see the children:

- Climbing to the top of a hill thinking that they would be able to see all the way to America,
- Being taught by their parents to read at home before being allowed to go to school,
- Having to carry their small lambs across a stream,
- Crying as they said good-bye to their beautiful valley, which they knew they would never see again.

I know that they walked 100 miles to Oslo, the capital of Norway, and that they stopped along the way to stay with strangers who told them how wonderful it was that they were going to America. I know that they went to a grand church in the capital city and heard a pipe organ playing the most beautiful music they'd ever heard.

Because Thora wrote her story, I not only know her name, I also know quite a bit about the kind of woman she was: what she loved, what she feared, and what she hoped for. My life and the world are richer because she took the time to sit down and write down her own story.

In the last year, as I've been traveling around the country publicizing my book, The Million Dollar Woman, I've had the opportunity to meet hundreds — if not thousands — of people from all walks of life. About eighty percent of the people I meet say things to me like this:

- "I've always wanted to write a book."
- "I have an idea for a book."
- "I started a book…"
- "When I was a kid, I dreamed about being an author."

Each person also shares with me the reasons why they haven't written the book they say they would like to write. Those explanations fall into four basic categories:

1. "I'm too busy, or I don't have the time."
2. "I don't know how to get started."
3. "It's too hard."
4. "I'm not smart enough."

In my opinion, these reasons all center on not knowing **how to write a book.** In other words, these people simply lack a quick and easy system — or method — for doing something they would like to do.

I used to be just like them. I wanted to write a book, but I wasn't sure I could actually do it. When I wrote my first book in 1994, it took me a whole year. Since that time, I've designed and refined my own system for writing a book to the point where I can begin and complete a book in five weeks. My system has an easy way to get started, an easy way to keep moving forward, and an easy way to keep writing all the way to the end.

In my "Write Your Own Book Club"™ Curriculum — which you can read about on my website: www.bobbimckenna.com — I give Book Club members a quick and easy way to write a non-fiction book.

But in this book, Telling Your Story™, I will focus entirely on helping you tell your own story in a way that not only forms a personal history, a legacy, and an identity, but also increases your understanding of the power of stories in your life and the lives of people you love.

A lot of people have told me that their story isn't important enough to write — as though there were some kind of "Special Commission" that must rate the merits of your story before you can write it.

Let me say once and for all: **You don't need anyone else's permission to write a book, or to tell your story.** It's your story, and it's your right to tell it. It is, after all, the most important story you could ever write!

Chapter One
IF YOU DON'T TELL YOUR STORY, WHO WILL?
"Winners All Have Strong Stories"

If you don't tell your story, one of two things will happen. Either your story will never be told, or if it's told at all, it probably won't be told in the way you want it told. It's that simple.

Human beings were made to tell stories. Stories tell us who we are, and what our lives mean. Stories tell us what we value and what we need. Without stories, we live disconnected, incomprehensible lives of isolation.

Stories are the blueprints we use to build our lives. Stories form our worldview, and our worldview shapes our stories. When external events seem to prove our stories false, we are rocked to our foundations. Until we can replace our old stories with new stories, we wander aimlessly, or collapse into a heap of self-doubt.

Stories tell us who we are, and it is at the times when our stories seem to fail us that we are most vulnerable to the negative, destructive stories that others tell. You know the kind of stories I'm talking about — the stories that tell us we're too young or too old to follow our dreams. The stories that tell us we're not smart enough, or good enough, or strong enough. The stories that scream, "You can't!"

We're all too familiar with the poisonous stories that are conveyed in words, and frowns, and smirks. The toxic stories that are told behind our backs and to our faces. I'm always amazed when I overhear someone saying: "I wouldn't say anything behind your back that I wouldn't say to your face" — as though cruelty is better when you hear its words and see its face "up close and personal." In my opinion, cruelty is cruelty, and cruelty seen close up is the worst cruelty of all.

Our external world is filled with all kinds of stories. Most of them are insidious, limiting stories that seek to enter our hearts and souls and keep us small and disappointed. They are stories that will diminish us if we believe them, and hold us back from our true greatness. The only way we can shield our hearts from these destructive stories is by making and keeping our own stories so strong and positive that they can withstand the assault!

In any conflict between people or cultures, the one with the strongest story always wins. To make your story strong, you must know what it is. Every story has a beginning, a middle, and an end. To know your story, you must know the beginning. Not every detail, because that's not possible for most of us. But the general outlines. Where you came from, and who came before you.

If you were adopted, like my daughter was, your story is even richer, even if you don't know every detail of it. One set of parents gave you life, and another set of parents took you into their hearts. You can draw from two rich heritages if you choose to do so.

For most of us, the first story we know is the story given to us by our parents. We come into the world, tender, unshaped, and open to receive whatever story we are told. Many of us are greeted with love, hope, and joy, mingled with some sense of uncertainty. Others of us are met with fear, and some even face violence.

When we are tiny, most of us accept, to some extent, the story we are told. Some of us are told that we were beautiful and brilliant. Others are told that we are ugly and stupid. As we grow, and mature, we can revisit those stories that we were told — those stories that we may still half believe.

We can look at those stories with adult eyes and realize that they are just stories. They are not composed entirely of objective facts. They are subjective descriptions of experience that were created by human beings — with human flaws and imperfections — who told your story in light of their own. The wounds they carried in their hearts were transferred to you.

With that perspective, you can take another look at those stories, and reshape them. You can rewrite them to fit the facts, as you know them today.

The story you choose to tell yourself about the beginning of your life will shape everything else that you do. Always choose the story that helps you. Always choose the story that serves you over the story that doesn't.

This book is designed so that you can record the stories that have shaped your life and your family's life. The first intent is to make sure that your heritage, your legacy, and your story, as you want it told, can be passed on to your children and their children. The second intent is to give you an opportunity to recall, revisit, and in some cases, reinterpret the stories that have shaped you and that still exert power over you. You can choose to loosen the grip of the stories that are holding you back, and pulling you down, and to strengthen the stories that will uplift you and carry you forward to your true greatness.

I have written an abbreviated version of my own story so that you can see how I have used the power of storytelling in my own life. The chapters are laid out in a chronological sequence that follows my own life. For instance, in my case I had children before I began my career, and then I had more children later, in mid-career. Many of you began your careers before you had children.

Some of you don't have children or aren't married. I adopted a child, which may apply to some or you and not to others. Some of you have faced life-threatening illnesses, the death of a spouse, or the loss of a child. I have been married only once, and have never been divorced. Even though divorce, remarriage, life-threatening illness, and loss of a spouse, a child, or a brother and sister are not a part of my story, I've included sections in the back of the book for you to use if they are part of your story.

Some of you may be at the beginning of your adult life, and you can begin recording your story now. As you move through life, you can use this book as a guide to writing your story. Feel free to use the sections of the book that relate to your own life and skip the ones that do not.

There are many details of my story that I've left out in this telling of my story — not because they weren't true, but because they wouldn't serve any useful purpose. This book isn't really about me. It's about you.

Look at this book as an opportunity to "Tell Your Own Story" in a way that helps you build the life you want.

Now, anyone who knows me will tell you that I'm a big fan of honesty. That's true, but while I greatly value honesty, I don't value "brutal" honesty. "Brutal" honesty rarely advances our cause, whatever it may be, or our understanding of any situation. It isn't hard to see why.

The definitions of the word "Brutal" given in the Random House Unabridged Dictionary are "cruel, inhuman, crude, coarse, harsh, ferocious, taxing, demanding, exhausting, irrational, and unreasoning." Its synonyms are "ferocious, brutish, barbarous, cruel, gross, rude, rough, uncivil, and bestial." Its antonyms are "kind and human."

I encourage you to avoid brutal honesty in the story you tell in the pages of this book, and the story you carry in your heart.

"Brutal" honesty will not bring you the life you desire and deserve. Instead, I encourage you to employ honesty that is "kind" and honesty that is "human." Use love and hope as your guiding stars, and write a strong story that will serve you well in the years ahead. Write your story so that it, and your life, will be a blessing to those you love and to the world.

I truly believe that the success of any venture is determined by the purity of the intentions. With that in mind, I urge you to purify your intentions and to tell yourself a story that will be worthy of your best self

_____

_____

_____

_____

_____

_____

_____

_____

_____

_____

_____

_____

_____

_____

_____

_____

_____

_____

_____

_____

_____

_____

_____

Chapter Two
WHERE I CAME FROM
"Everything's More Fun When You're Wearing Pink Plastic Rhinestone Studded Sunglasses!"

The Norwegian side of my family came to the United States from Norway in the Nineteen Century. My grandfather's family set sail from Norway in 1871. The first time they set out, a storm washed their water barrels overboard, and without fresh water to drink, they had to turn back. They bought new barrels, filled them with water and set out again for a land they had never seen. The children went out onto the deck of the ship to see the high fiords of Norway receding in the distance. There was calm weather for a few days and then, according to my Great Aunt, Thora Franklin, "a terrible storm came, but God stilled the storm."

My grandfather, Tom Franklin, was a young child when he came to America, and my father told me that he spoke English without an accent. My grandmother, Elise Pedersen, got on a ship when she was only sixteen years old. Accompanied only by her seventeen-year old brother, Kris, she sailed off to find a better life. She left her parents in Lillehammer, Norway, but her father Frans Pedersen later came to America.

I recount these details to show how a personal story is crafted from such small facts. My story as I have told it to myself begins with people who were courageous, undaunted by adversity, and willing to risk their lives to follow their dream. That is my story.

Another person might take the same facts and create a story in which poor people were forced to leave their homes and risk their lives on the high seas. How you tell the story makes all the difference, doesn't it?

What about your family? Where did they come from? What are the stories that people in your family tell each other about who you are?

Although I am an only child, my father, Obert Franklin, was one of ten children, and so my extended family is very large. My family practices what I call "Extreme Togetherness." If it were an Olympic Sport, my family would win a Gold Medal.

As Lori, my cousin Vern's wife, puts it: "This family goes everywhere in a mob. When I was being wheeled into the delivery room for my daughter's birth, there they all were. The whole Franklin clan."

We're not talking about six or seven people going to a movie. We're talking about anywhere from forty to sixty people — loud, flamboyant people going to the Sizzler on Ocean Beach Highway in Longview, Washington for dinner. We're talking about fifty people taking over the Pantry Restaurant just down the street from the Big Chicken. For holidays or birthdays, we rent a hall like the Son's of Norway, and everyone dances, even the kids. Sometimes we have theme parties and everyone dresses up like it's 1958 with poodle skirts and retro "cat's eye-pink-plastic-rhinestone-studded" glasses. When I was growing up, I thought "pink-plastic-rhinestone-studded" was one word. Those were the days when my Aunt Bessie and my Aunt Adeline owned and operated the Chinook Fountain in downtown Kalama, not far from the totem pole carved by Chief Lalooska.

The Chinook Fountain was your classic Hamburger, Fries, Milkshakes, and Cherry Coke kind of hangout with pinball machines and a jukebox. I got to work behind the counter, plunging frozen strips of potato into the deep fryer and watching as the white potatoes turned golden — okay, so sometimes I forgot about them, and they turned into incinerated ashen twigs instead of elegant droopy fries. I whipped up shakes in the mixer and then poured them into frosted glasses. Boys who looked like "Fonzie" came in and gave me money for the jukebox. It was just like Happy Days.

Years later, when my own children were young, I wanted them to experience the small town version of life, where every second person you met was a cousin, or an uncle, or somehow related by marriage. I would buy plane tickets and we would travel across the country from Washington, D.C. to Longview, Washington to attend "The Thunder Mountain Pro Rodeo" with my family. Some, but not all, family members dress up for the rodeo like they're starring in a Spaghetti Western. As a result, my children swear, to this day, that everyone in my family is a cowboy. They've got hundreds of snapshots to prove it.

"Look," they say, "There's Grandpa in his cowboy hat and cowboy boots."

Grandpa (my dad) was six feet four in his cowboy boots, and wearing a big silver belt buckle on his belt, he looked just like Clint Eastwood in "Unforgiven."

One of my friends, Bob, an attorney from New York City, went to the Oregon Coast with me and met some of my family. When he came to Colorado to visit us, he was approached by a mutual friend, an attorney from Colorado also named Bob. — Have you ever wondered why there are so many Bobs and why so many of them are attorneys? — Anyway, the Bob from Colorado asked the Bob from New York City, "What's Bobbi's family like?"

"They're funny," the Bob from New York City said.

His reply didn't surprise me. I smiled and nodded. You see, the Credo of my family consists of two parts: The first part is that we are the wittiest family on the face of the earth. The second part is that we have more fun than any other family, and we have the evidence to prove it.

With so many family members, we have a party almost every week. It's always someone's birthday. At every gathering, we spend most of our time repeating all the funny stories from the past, all the while telling each other how much fun we're having and how unbelievably funny we are. We are certain that we are the envy of other families, who cannot possibly be having as much fun as we are.

But I digress. As I was saying, the first Bob, the lawyer from New York City, had just said that my family was funny. The second Bob, the lawyer from Colorado, was narrowing his eyes, and was mulling over the meaning of the word funny.

"Funny, ha-ha?" he asked. "Or funny eccentric?"

"Uh…" The first Bob began to sweat and reached up to loosen the collar of his shirt. He shot a glance my way, licked his lips, and then uttered the words that have been the source of much merriment in my family. "Uh," he croaked. "Uh…eccentric."

I was wounded. "What do you mean? I asked.

"Well, there was THAT WOMAN," he said, clearly sweating now, gulping from his wine glass.

"Which woman?" I asked.

"The one with the dog," he said grabbing the wine bottle and rushing out to the patio to smoke a cigarette.

The "one with the dog" would be Aunt Eldora, the wittiest member of my family. She's a cross between Carol Burnett and Lily Tomlin. She's also a seventy-five year old bowling champion who goes to Reno to gamble on her birthday, lives with her dog Johnny Franklin (a Cockapoo,) and too many cats to count in a tiny white house. ECCENTRIC? — I think not!

I call her later to tell her what this attorney named Bob from New York City has said about her. She laughs so hard that she can't speak. When she regains her poise, she says, "Well, I guess if he comes to the beach again, I'll just have to bury him in the sand." She's laughing so hard when she says this that I can hardly make out the words.

Now, some of you may be wondering why a loving niece would repeat a derogatory comment to her aunt. In my family, we take it as a matter pride that the rest of the world may not "get" who we are because we are just so cool. We also assume that other families are consumed with envy.

It would never cross our minds that any family would not want to be exactly like us — if only they had the talent and charm to pull it off. (I once overheard my husband — who worships the ground I walk on — telling a group of people that my family is just like the people portrayed in the movie "Fargo." I don't think he meant it as a compliment, but that's the way my family and I choose to take it.)

There are many advantages to belonging to a family that thinks it is always having fun. The biggest advantage is the low incidence and low intensity of conflict. Let me describe to you the only "fight" I can ever recall occurring in my family. It happened fourteen years ago when I was in town to attend my Aunt Bessie's 80th Birthday Party. I wanted three of my Aunts to go with me to Astoria for lunch. (You may remember Astoria from the movie Kindergarten Cop, which starred a man who later became the Governor of California.) Anyway, my Aunt Mabel was talking on the phone to her baby sister, Aunt Eldora, she of eccentric fame.

I heard Aunt Mabel quietly say, "All right then, Goodbye."

She hung up the phone, turned to me, and said, "She — just — won't—make — up — her — mind." Aunt Mabel speaks softly even when she is boiling mad, but she puts spaces between her words for emphasis. She also calls her husband, Ed, "MIS-

TER," when she's hot under the collar, but that's another story.

"I was so mad," Aunt Mabel takes a breath, "that I just said, 'All right then, Goodbye.'"

This was the big fight in my family.

The reason I include this "altercation" in my book is to demonstrate just how powerful the stories that we tell ourselves can be. In my family, we tell ourselves that we are always happy, that we are the funniest, happiest family on earth, that we have more fun than anybody else, and BECAUSE WE BELIEVE THESE THINGS, THEY BECOME TRUE FOR US.

This is our family creed. This is the map we follow. This is our reality.

Our favorite stories are about the annual Fourth of July picnics that everyone has attended for almost sixty years, the vacation at the beach when someone went into labor, the many occasions when the seventy year old aunts fell down the steep riverbank when they were picking wild blackberries and we all laughed at them, the way Grandma Elisa sang the "Here Comes the Sandman Song" in her Norwegian accent when she rocked us to sleep, and then we repeat some of the things she said to us —things like: "Have a 'Yelly' sandwich." (Jelly sandwich.) And "You'd better stop 'yumping' up and down on the bed!" There are so many stories that they would fill thirty books, and all of the stories are filled with laughter.

What are the stories your family lives by? If you had to sum them up in a few sentences, what would you say? And what effect do those stories have on you?

Turn the page and write down everything you know about the people who came before you in your family. Go back as far as you can, but don't wait until you've had time to do research. If you wait until you have time to find out everything you could possibly know, you'll never start writing. If you discover something that you want to explore in more depth, do it later, after you've finished writing the rest of your story. You can always add things, and expand sections, but for now, you need to begin. (There will be a separate chapter each for your mother and father so don't include them in this section.)

Many of us only know our family names going back to our Great-Great Grandparents if that far. If you have a lengthy family tree that goes back further than that, you may use the note pages in the back of the book to record their names.

Father's Family

Great, Great, Great Grandparents

_____ _____

_____ _____

_____ _____

_____ _____

Great, Great, Great Grandparents

_____ _____

_____ _____

_____ _____

_____ _____

Great, Great Grandparents

_____

_____

_____

_____

Great, Great Grandparents

_____

_____

_____

_____

Great Grandparents

_____

_____

Great Grandparents

_____

_____

Your Grandmother

_____

Your Grandfather

_____

Your Father

_____

You

_____

Stories

If you wanted me to know your father's family, what are the five most significant and characteristic stories you would tell me?

1. _____

_____

_____

_____

_____

_____

_____

_____

_____

_____

_____

_____

_____

_____

2. _____

_____

_____

_____

_____

_____

_____

_____

_____

_____

_____

_____

_____

_____

_____

_____

3. _____

_____

_____

_____

_____

_____

_____

_____

_____

_____

_____

_____

_____

_____

_____

_____

_____

4. _____

_____

_____

_____

_____

_____

_____

_____

_____

_____

_____

_____

_____

_____

_____

5. _____

_____

_____

_____

_____

_____

_____

_____

_____

_____

_____

_____

_____

_____

_____

_____

If you had to sum up to a friend what your father's family creed is, what would it be?

_____

_____

_____

_____

_____

_____

_____

Mother's Family

Great, Great, Great Grandparents

_____ _____

_____ _____

_____ _____

_____ _____

Great, Great, Great Grandparents

_____ _____

_____ _____

_____ _____

_____ _____

Great, Great Grandparents

_____

_____

_____

_____

Great, Great Grandparents

_____

_____

_____

_____

Great Grandparents

_____

_____

Great Grandparents

_____

_____

Your Grandmother

_____

Your Grandfather

_____

Your Mother

_____

You

_____

Stories

If you wanted someone to know your mother's family, what are the five most significant and characteristic stories you would tell him or her?

1. _____

_____

_____

_____

_____

_____

_____

_____

_____

_____

_____

_____

_____

_____

_____

_____

_____

_____

_____

_____

2. _____

_____

_____

_____

_____

_____

_____

_____

_____

_____

_____

_____

_____

_____

_____

_____

_____

_____

_____

_____

_____

3. _____

_____

_____

_____

_____

_____

_____

_____

_____

_____

_____

_____

_____

_____

_____

_____

_____

_____

_____

_____

_____

4. _____

_____

_____

_____

_____

_____

_____

_____

_____

_____

_____

_____

_____

_____

_____

_____

_____

_____

_____

_____

5. _____

_____

_____

_____

_____

_____

_____

_____

_____

_____

_____

_____

_____

_____

_____

_____

_____

_____

If you had to sum up to a friend what your mother's family creed is, what would it be?

_____

_____

_____

_____

_____

Chapter Three
FATHER
"Fishing, Banjos, and Cowboy Boots"

My father, Obert (Robert without the "R") Franklin, was born in a small farmhouse on the plains of North Dakota. In our family lexicon we call it "the little house on the prairie." My dad had eight brothers and sisters, and one older stepbrother. My father told me that his father was a successful farmer, but his farm was limited in size by the farms of his two brothers. He wanted more land, and so he sold his farm and moved further west to homestead. Shortly after the move, he developed Parkinson's Disease, and the family struggled from then on, with barely enough money to live on. By the time my father was born, his father was ill and was 55 years old.

As he put it, "When I was born, my dad, Tom Franklin, was already an old man, sick in bed."

One story my father told me over and over was that one day, his dad had called him to his bedside and had given him a knife that he had received from his own father.

"My Dad thought a lot of that knife," my father told me. "I went out to play, and somehow I lost it. It must have fallen from my pocket. I looked everywhere. I went through every piece of hay in the barn. I stayed out until dark, looking for it in the weeds and the dirt, but I never found it."

I could hear the shame in my father's voice. That knife had been the only treasure that a sick man had been able to give to his son. The knife was more than a knife. It was a blessing, and my father knew — even in his child's heart — that he had let that blessing fall through his fingers.

"It hurt me worse than anything to have to go back and tell my Dad that I had lost the knife his own father gave him," he told me.

Those were the kinds of stories — stories of loss — that became my father's map. It didn't matter that my father was tall and handsome. It didn't matter that he was smart, and that when he walked into a room and flashed his glorious smile, everyone loved him. All that mattered was that because his father had wanted more, "he had lost everything." All that mattered was that "when he had been given the knife that was to be his legacy, he ran out to play and lost it."

My dad graduated from high school just as the Second World War broke out. He enlisted in the Seabees because he didn't want to kill anyone, and the Seabees were just supposed to build things. As he told me, "They forgot to tell me that we had to build things so the Marines could land." He served in the South Pacific and spent one leave in Australia, which he always recalled with pleasure. He came home from the war, and won a scholarship to go to college, but like so many of his generation, he took a job and got married instead.

At most of the pivot points in his life, my father looked at the world through the prism of those stories of loss, and he shied away from risks like a skittish horse at the edge of riverbank.

When I was a child, I didn't understand any of these things. He was tall and handsome. He could sing and dance, and he looked like a male model or a movie star. He had a great laugh, and he winked when he smiled. I got his smile, and his voice, and his wink.

He would push me in my swing and carry me inside and put me to bed when I fell asleep in the car. Sometimes I pretended that I was asleep just so I could feel his strong arms around me.

Without a son, I was the one he took hunting and fishing. Some of my happiest memories are of fishing for rainbow trout in a fast-running, clear mountain stream, or standing on the bridge at Multnomah Falls feeling the spray from the falls on my face.

We went to the beach every chance we got. We went to Cannon Beach and climbed Haystock Rock — the third largest freestanding volcanic formation in the world. We almost got caught by the tide every single time. The desperate, headlong rush down the craggy volcanic rock and the wild dash through the waves to the safety of the hard wet sand was the most fun part of the adventure.

We rode horses through the surf, and at low tide, we waded in the Devil's Punch Bowl — a collapsed volcanic structure north of Newport. I scooped handfuls of agates into my bucket while he stacked driftwood into a windbreak. Years later, when I was an adult, I discovered that he didn't even like the beach because he hated to have the wind blowing in his face. (To those of you who don't know, if you don't want the wind blowing in your face, you shouldn't go to the Oregon Coast.) He spent all that time at the beach because I loved the beach, and he loved me.

My dad was a big kid through and through. He could sing like a troubadour and play the banjo all night. He loved to dance: the Fox Trot, the Jitter Bug, and then, later in life square dancing.

He carried a toothpick between his gleaming white teeth with the same swagger that Bogart held a cigarette in his mouth when he talked. He was the sun and the moon and the stars to me. He was my Dad. But when I won a scholarship to college on the other side of the country, he couldn't understand why I would want to go.

"Why do you want to leave your old dad?" he asked me. "You'll fall in love with some boy back East, and never see your old dad anymore." He was forty-three years old at the time.

When I left to go away to college, I was rejecting his stories — the stories that he had lived by, and that he would continue to live by. I didn't want to hurt him, but I couldn't content myself with stories of loss and fear. I had to choose my own stories — stories where taking risks leads not to loss, but to triumph, and the only shame comes from not trying to do great things.

As my dad predicted, I did fall in love with a boy back East, and seven years later, I was in Korea with my husband and baby, when my father suffered a heart attack. He was among the first group of cardiac patients to undergo quadruple bypass surgery. Sadly, his health was never robust again.

We did have one more wonderful week together after I returned from Korea. I had two babies by then, and he came to visit me in Washington, DC. We went to Arlington Cemetery where so many of the young men he'd shipped out with to the South Pacific had been buried. We had lunches at what he called "chi-chi French restaurants" in Georgetown. One lunch featured a shouting match between one of my friends who was a reporter at the Washington Post and one of my graduate school professors from George Washington University.

As the years went by, my father enjoyed my children at the rodeo, but he and I were never quite in sync again. We loved each other, but we couldn't find any common ground.

As he grew older, he became increasingly racially intolerant. I couldn't spend ten minutes talking to him without being drawn into an argument that would result in my having to remove my children from his presence. And yet, when my aunt called and told me that my Dad had died, I broke down and sobbed like a baby.

I'd always known I would experience a sense of loss when he was gone — and that I would grieve — but I found his death unsettling in ways I hadn't expected. It was like having a continent that had always been there suddenly disappear from the map. I spent a long summer and autumn, dealing with a sense of dislocation and disorientation. Gradually, I redrew the map and rewrote my story. But the sense of loss, while less intense, will always remain.

I'm very blessed to have all those happy memories of the times my dad and I spent together. I can hear his laugh, and I can see traces of him in myself and in my children. If you still have your dad with you, enjoy the time with him as much as possible. Write this chapter in your story so that you will have it to comfort you through the years ahead.

~   ~   ~

Write down as many facts as you can about your father's life.

_____

Your Father's Name, Place and Date of Birth

Names of his brothers and sisters:

_____

_____

Schools he attended and the years he graduated:

_____

Subjects he loved:

_____

Sports he played:

_____

_____

_____

Military Service: Branch and Dates of Service, Medals

_____

Marriages: Location, Date, and Name of Spouse(s)

_____

Names and dates of birth of all children:

_____

Write down the five stories your father told you about his life that you believe shaped his understanding of himself and his place in the world:

1. _____

_____

_____

_____

_____

_____

_____

_____

_____

_____

_____

_____

_____

_____

2. _____

_____

_____

_____

_____

_____

_____

_____

_____

_____

_____

_____

_____

3. _____

_____

_____

_____

_____

_____

_____

_____

_____

_____

_____

_____

_____

4. _____

_____

_____

_____

_____

_____

_____

_____

_____

_____

_____

_____

5. _____

_____

_____

_____

_____

_____

_____

_____

_____

_____

_____

_____

_____

_____

Write down your five favorite stories about your father:

1. _____

_____

_____

_____

_____

_____

_____

_____

_____

_____

_____

_____

_____

_____

_____

_____

_____

_____

_____

2. _____

_____

_____

_____

_____

_____

_____

_____

_____

_____

_____

_____

_____

_____

_____

3. _____

4. _____

_____

_____

_____

_____

_____

_____

_____

_____

_____

_____

_____

_____

_____

_____

5. _____

_____

_____

_____

_____

_____

_____

_____

_____

_____

_____

_____

_____

_____

_____

_____

_____

_____

_____

How have the stories he told you affected you?

_____

_____

_____

_____

_____

_____

_____

_____

_____

_____

_____

_____

_____

_____

_____

How have the stories you tell yourself about him affected you?

_____

_____

_____

_____

_____

_____

_____

_____

_____

If you have lost your father, write about that here. What happened and how you have processed losing him and made it part of your story:

_____

_____

_____

_____

_____

_____

_____

_____

_____

_____

_____

_____

_____

_____

_____

_____

_____

_____

_____

Chapter Four
MOTHER
"French Twists, Caviar, And Hawaiian Sunsets On The Lanai"

My mother, Jean Bowen, was born in Jamestown, North Dakota. She was one of a family of two children. Her mother was of Welsh Irish descent and her father was Irish. By the time my mother was born, her parents had already separated, and her father had moved away. I don't think she ever met him. My grandmother, Vera, remarried and her new husband was a devoted stepfather. My mother was pretty, very smart, and everyone doted on her.

She was 5'4," had blue eyes and strawberry blond hair, which she liked to wear in a French Twist. She had a taste for all the finer things: Crystal, antiques, caviar, and elegant clothes. She loved champagne, and always shopped at Nordstrom's. She went to Hawaii on her second honeymoon, and every balcony or patio she ever set foot on after that, she referred to as "the Lanai." She wore very high heels, and she was a career woman in the days of "Ozzie and Harriet" and "Leave It To Beaver." Her first car was a Pontiac, and when she made right turns, she sometimes scraped the side of her door up against a telephone pole.

When she was in high school, she studied Latin. She wanted to be a dancer, and she wanted to be very rich. She wanted everything. She loved movies, and identified with the life she saw in them. My father looked like a movie star, and he could sing like Bing Crosby, so she married him.

It's a recipe for disaster when a woman who wants everything (no matter what the risks) marries a man who wants nothing more than safety. When I was born, she was happy to have a baby, but she didn't want any more children.

The first formative stories my mother told me were:
1. Hers was the worst pregnancy any woman had ever endured.
2. I was two months overdue (which I believe is a biological impossibility) and,
3. Her labor was the longest labor the doctors and nurses had ever seen.

The second set of formative stories my mother told me were:
1. When I was born I had a round face, was pretty, and looked like her, but
2. Somewhere around the age of three or four, my face narrowed and lengthened, and (Horror!) I began to look like my father.

By the time I was seven or eight, she was beginning a mental deterioration that would continue throughout the rest of her life. Her illness didn't turn her into a bewildered, vague woman in a sheer nightgown. Instead, it made her angry and abusive.

I would give almost anything to be able to tell a different story here because I know that it makes people feel uncomfortable to hear it. I've spent most of my life not telling this part of my story, and I've agonized over my decision to include it in this book. Believe me, I would rather leave it out. In fact, as I typed those words, I considered hitting the delete key and sweeping it all away. But I've included my story in this book only to serve as a model for you as you write your story. If I'm not willing to risk being vulnerable, I'm not setting a very good example for you.

You may be wondering if my mother received mental health treatment. Yes, she saw psychiatrists, but she only saw each one for a month or two before he or she would refuse to see her anymore or take her calls. She was very intelligent and manipulative, and so difficult that ultimately, there was not a single psychiatrist in Portland, Oregon who would have anything to do with her.

She couldn't be helped because she didn't think she had a problem. She thought that all the rest of us had a problem: My dad, my step-dad, my grandmother, the psychiatrists, and I. In a way, she was absolutely right.

There were drug overdoses, middle of the night visits from the police, and an episode which ended in gunfire. As my mother's illness progressed, she bombarded me with negative stories for the simple reason that I was there, close at hand. Because I was a child, I couldn't get away from her. I heard her words, but I knew that I didn't have to believe them. They were her words and her stories, not mine, and so I created and told myself stories of goodness, virtue, and honor.

As a small child, I learned to distinguish between those things we can control and those we cannot. I did not get to choose my mother, but I did get to choose my reaction to my mother. She had the power to make my childhood and adolescence miserable, but I refused to give her the power to control my future.

If I succumbed to anger, resentment, or depression, I would be letting her and her stories win. The only way I could win was to make my stories stronger than her stories.

According to the stories I told myself, I did not have to be content with what life had handed me. I could believe in a better life. I could work for it. I could reach for it. I could bring it into being by doing the right thing, being the best I could be, working hard, reaching for every high branch, taking every risk, and never taking "no" for an answer.

Because my home wasn't a refuge from the world, the world became my refuge. Eventually, I escaped physically from my mother, but I never felt completely safe from her until the day she died.

She died the way she lived: in chaos. She took an overdose of prescription drugs one too many times. None of the people she had instructed to "check on her" remembered to do it, and she slipped from her drugged sleep into a deep sleep where I pray she has found the peace she never knew in this life.

I would love to be able to tell a different kind of story here, but I can't. This is the truth about my mother, but it isn't the "brutal" truth. There is much that I left out of this account. The only comfort I feel about including any of it is that some of you who are reading this book may gain the courage to tell the truth about the painful parts of your own stories, whatever they may be.

Most of you have wonderful stories to tell about your mother, and this is the place where you can record those stories. If your mother is still with you, I encourage you to write new chapters in your story together, and fill these chapters with meaning and joy.

Write down as many facts as you can about your mother's life including place and date of birth:

_____

Names of her brothers and sisters:

_____

_____

Schools she attended and the year she graduated:

_____

Subjects she loved:

_____

Sports she played:

_____

_____

Military Service if applicable:

_____

Marriages: Location, Date, and Name of Spouse(s)

_____

Names and dates of birth of all children

Write down the five stories your mother told you about her life that you believe shaped her understanding of herself and her place in the world:

1. _____

_____

_____

_____

_____

_____

_____

_____

_____

_____

_____

_____

_____

2. _____

_____

_____

_____

_____

_____

_____

_____

_____

_____

_____

_____

_____

3. _____

_____

_____

_____

_____

_____

_____

_____

_____

_____

_____

_____

4. _____

_____

_____

_____

_____

_____

_____

_____

_____

_____

_____

_____

_____

5. _____

_____

_____

_____

_____

_____

_____

_____

_____

_____

_____

Write down your five favorite stories about your mother:

1. _____

_____

_____

_____

_____

_____

_____

_____

_____

_____

_____

_____

_____

_____

_____

_____

_____

2. _____

_____

_____

_____

_____

_____

_____

_____

_____

_____

_____

_____

_____

_____

_____

_____

3. _____

_____

_____

_____

_____

_____

_____

_____

_____

_____

4. _____

5. _____

_____

_____

_____

_____

_____

_____

_____

_____

_____

_____

_____

_____

_____

_____

_____

_____

_____

How have the stories she told you affected you?

_____

_____

_____

_____

_____

_____

_____

_____

How have the stories you tell yourself about her affected you?

_____

_____

_____

_____

_____

_____

_____

If you have lost your mother, write about that here. Write about what happened, and tell how you have processed losing her and made it a part of your story:

_____

_____

_____

_____

_____

_____

_____

_____

_____

_____

_____

_____

_____

_____

_____

_____

_____

_____

_____

_____

Chapter Five
CHILDHOOD
"Skinned Knees, Puppy Dogs, and Long Days at the Beach"

Where to begin? It's my theory that childhood is to blame for most of our feelings of low self-esteem. No matter how big, strong, rich, powerful, successful, brilliant, beautiful, or handsome we become later in life, most of us operate out of the self-image we form in the classrooms, hallways, and playgrounds of elementary school. Every person I've ever talked to about their childhood remembers it as a time of at least some humiliation and torment.

Most of us still have moments when we feel as awkward and powerless as we did as a child when we were picked last for something. It only had to happen once in order to leave a searing scar on our psyches. A hundred successes carry less emotional power for us than a single rejection. In general, we remember the slights and disappointments much more vividly than we remember the high points. At least that's my theory.

We're either too tall, or too short. We're either too fat, or too skinny. Some of us are timid. We begin to interact with other children at a time when we don't have complete control over all of our bodily functions. Our noses run, our shoelaces come untied. We lose our boots and our lunch money. Where does it end?

When I was little, there wasn't any nursery school. I had to stay at home with Margie, my babysitter, until I was old enough to go to kindergarten. I played by myself most of the time, listened to the radio, read books, sang and practiced writing my alphabet. Sometimes I played with the little girl next door.

I wanted to be a movie star, and one rainy holiday when the whole Franklin clan was jammed into Grandma's house, the grownups made the big kids take the little kids to the movies. I was one of the little kids: five years old.

It was my favorite kind of movie: singing, dancing, and kissing. I was sitting next to my cousin Greg. I saw Doris Day up there on the big screen, singing and dancing, and I was certain I could do it just as well as she was doing it. I slipped out of my seat. Greg asked me where I was going.

"Up there," I said, pointing at the stage.

"You'd better not!" he said. "You'll get in trouble."

I was already moving down the aisle, over to the right side of the stage where the steps would take me up to the movie. Five steps, and I was up there on the stage. I walked right out to the middle, held my arms straight out at my sides the way Shirley Temple did in the old movies, and I began to sing. Midway through my song, one of the older cousins had to come and drag me off the stage, but I didn't care. I had sung in the movie

When it finally came time for me to go to kindergarten, the local elementary school was being remodeled and the children in our neighborhood had to be bussed to another school. Some genius decided it would be too hard on the kindergarten children to have to ride a school bus, and so we were given a classroom in the nearby High School. Unbelievable!

I had to walk across the huge football field every day to get to school. One day it rained so had that the field turned into a swamp. I got stuck in the middle, right around the fifty-yard line, and I fell down. When I tried to get up, my boots came off and I had to walk the rest of the way in my little Orthopedic

Mary Jane shoes and white anklets. I looked like the "Abominable Mud Midget" by the time I got to school. We're talking thick, slick, slimy mud!

The worst thing about kindergarten was that the teacher wouldn't let me go to the bathroom when I needed to. Her bathroom break schedule and my bladder were in conflict, and I also seem to recall that she had some kind of fetish about how many paper towels I should use to dry my hands after I washed them.

About midway through the kindergarten year, my parents bought a house, and while they got it ready for us to live in, I stayed with my mother's mother, Grandma Vera.

Grandma Vera wore sundresses and shoes with open toes and wedge heels. She drove a Nash Rambler, and let me listen to the opera on the radio. My Uncle John, who still lived at home, stayed out late at night, and slept most of the day. I had to go to a new kindergarten.

In this kindergarten, we had naptime. We could get up from our nap when the teacher tapped us on the shoulder with a pink magic wand that she had. She said that she would choose the children who were very still and didn't move. I lay as still as I could. I held my breath so my body wouldn't move, but she never chose me first. In fact, I was usually one of the last to be tapped with the magic wand.

The day finally came when I could move into my new home with my parents. I went to a new school where I stayed for seven years. I was a good student, and I liked school. But life at school wasn't perfect.

I was too tall — taller than everyone else. I was even taller than the boys. My mother was the only who worked, and I was one of the few children who had to buy my lunch! I was also one of the first to get to school in the morning, and then I had to walk to daycare where I had to deal with boys who were bullies and pulled my hair. I was glad when I was finally old enough to stay home after school by myself and watch the Mickey Mouse Club.

I had a white rabbit, named Fluffy Bunny Franklin, who was so big that he chased big neighborhood dogs up the street. I sold greeting cards door to door, until I saved twenty dollars which was enough to buy a puppy. I went with my dad to a house that was selling puppies, and I picked out a fawn-colored Chihuahua. I named her "Pepsi Cola" or "Peppy" for short. She grew huge, so huge that after the rabbit died, she took over the job of chasing the big neighborhood dogs up the street.

These were also the years when Americans lived with the fear of nuclear holocaust every day. I remember worrying about whether the Soviets would bomb us. I would sit in school and plan how I would go home, get my bike, put my Chihuahua in the basket on the handlebars of my bike and ride out of town. In Portland, we had evacuation signs pointing which way we should go in case of nuclear attack. We also practiced for air raids, and went out into the hallway and stood facing our metal lockers, with our arms folded over our heads as though that would protect us from nuclear attack. I don't know about other people at the time, but I worried that I wouldn't get the chance to grow up, fall in love, get married, and have children before nuclear war ended all life on earth.

During my childhood and adolescence, legal segregation was dismantled. Growing up in Portland, Oregon in those years, I knew very few African Americans. I read Time Magazine and watched the news, but I don't remember any of this being discussed by my parents.

The people who said that you couldn't legislate morality were wrong. The laws changed, and as a consequence, people's behavior had to change. What you do defines who you are, and we are a better people today. As my friend John Alston says, "All people have problems. What's different about Americans is that we try to fix ours."

I did all the normal childhood things. Sports for girls weren't big then, but I was in Brownies and Girl Scouts, and I took baton twirling, but when I threw my baton in the air, I could never catch it.

Added to the fact that I was too tall, I also had a name, "Barbara Franklin," that the boys at school could cleverly rearrange into "Barbequed Frankfurter," or if they were too tired to say all that, they would simply shout at me: "Hey, Barbara Frankenstein."

My parents got divorced when I was ten, and it was okay at first, but then I was alone with my mom. She drank too much and started taking prescription medications. My childhood was over except for the time I spent with my Dad and his family.

Whenever we went to see her, my Grandmother Franklin would always come to the door, and say, "Oh, for heaven's sake!" in her Norwegian accent, like we had come from thousands of miles away instead of only fifty. She would cook for us, never sitting down at the table to eat. She would stand hovering over us at the table so that she could serve us more and more food. Fried fish, roast beef, mashed potatoes and gravy, and her sublime Lemon Chiffon pie.

Sometimes, she would also put her arm around my waist, look up at me and say, "Barbara Jean (pronounced like "yeen"), you're so terrible tall!" The word "terrible" in "Grandma Franklin lingo" meant "very," but I got the message. She also was concerned that no boy would ever grow tall enough to marry me. (On my wedding day I was 5'7" tall, and my husband was 6' tall.)

Grandma Franklin had a big TV in her living room, and she loved Englebert Humperdinck and the Beatles. I seem to recall her dancing with my cousin Greg and me, but I might have dreamed it.

American Bandstand was on TV, and I had a crush on our paperboy. He did not return my affections. My friends and I went to dancing classes, and sometimes we went down to the Portland, Oregon version of American Bandstand.

When I was in the eighth grade, my mother married a successful lawyer, and we moved to a beautiful new split level home on the side of a hill. I went to a new school, and even though I was still too tall and still wearing the orthopedic shoes my mother insisted on, I felt more at ease at school.

My mother's marriage lasted less than two months. It ended in gunfire, and eventually my mother and I moved again. No one was killed in the gunfire, but it was a little too close for comfort.

Most of my happiest childhood times were spent with my Dad and his family. I also loved music and singing, and I loved to swim and go to the beach. I had a bike, and I rode to my friends' houses. There were great parties with the Franklin Family band playing: Uncle Mickey on the fiddle, Dad on the guitar or banjo, and my cousins Jimmy, Ty, and Larry playing guitars.

While my childhood was not an idyllic childhood by any means, it was during those years that I turned to books to learn about the kind of life I wanted. It was also during my childhood that I began to tell myself the positive and inspiring stories that have enabled me to endure and overcome adversity throughout my life.

What are your first school memories?

_____

_____

_____

_____

_____

Who were your best childhood friends?

1. _____
2. _____
3. _____
4. _____
5. _____

What were your favorite activities?

1. _____
2. _____
3. _____
4. _____
5. _____

What are your favorite childhood memories?

1. _____

_____

_____

_____

_____

2. _____

_____

_____

_____

_____

3. _____

_____

_____

_____

_____

4. _____

_____

_____

_____

_____

5. _____

_____

_____

_____

_____

_____

How have the stories you tell yourself about your childhood affected you?

_____

_____

_____

_____

_____

_____

_____

_____

_____

ᕵ   ᕵ   ᕵ

Chapter Six
HIGH SCHOOL
"Proms, Plays, First Love, And Rock And Roll"

The pimple years! I was still too tall, although a lot of the boys were finally taller than I was. I was in "EE" classes (similar to what we call "Advanced Placement" classes today.) I had a great English teacher, who introduced me to Shakespeare. I took voice lessons, sang in the choir, and was active in drama.

I had a friend who played the guitar, and he and I formed a folk ensemble. We were "Peter, Paul, and Mary," without Paul. We performed at every given opportunity, and I also sang solos at other events.

I fell in love with one boy, but he regarded me as a friend. Another boy fell in love with me, and I regarded him as a friend. And that pretty much says it all about high school. I know there were people who loved high school. For some it was the high point of their lives, but not for me. I did learn to drive, but driving is actually not one of my favorite activities. My mom had a burgundy-colored Mustang, which I loved. My dad drove a Fire Engine Red Mustang, which he kept for thirty-five years.

I remember the day John F. Kennedy was assassinated. I had a lead in a play that was supposed to open the next night. I was sitting on the sofa in the drama room with other people who were in the play, when a boy named Irvin rushed into the room. Irvin was the clown of the drama department, and no one ever took him seriously.

"President Kennedy's been shot! President Kennedy's been shot!" he screamed.

"Oh, you're so full of it," one of the other guys said.

"It's true!" Irvin screamed.

"Sure, sure!" everyone said.

Not one of us believed Irvin. It was unthinkable that anyone would shoot the President. The bell rang, and I got up from the sofa, and went to my next class, which was choir.

I walked into the choir room, and the teacher said, "The President is dead."

I don't remember whether we were dismissed early, or if I went home at the regular time. School was cancelled the next day, and so was the play. I just remember walking around town with one of my friends. We were in a daze. If President Kennedy could be killed, it seemed like nothing made sense anymore and might never make sense again. When Jack Ruby shot Lee Harvey Oswald in the Dallas Police Station with all the policemen standing right there, the senselessness became surreal.

My husband, Bob, was a student at Georgetown University that November day. He was in Copley Hall getting ready to go to class when he heard that the President had been shot. He went to the Debate Team Office. Someone came in and said: "The President is dead!" Bob Shrum, who is now a famous political consultant, broke down completely. It was the only time my husband has ever seen Bob Shrum lose control. It rocked them all to their foundations.

As my husband says, "Georgetown was the great Catholic University, and John Kennedy was the first Catholic President."

Since Bob was in Washington, DC, he was able to go with his friends to see the cortege taking the body of the slain president from the White House to the Capitol. He was standing right on the curb of Pennsylvania Avenue as the cortege went by. He can still remember the haunting sound of the unaccompanied drums, going "Rat-tat-tat" over and over, and the gut-wrenching sight of the rider-less horse.

Other members of our extended family had close connections to that day. My youngest son's godfather was a young marine officer marching in that procession. Father Richard Mc Sorley, who baptized our second son, Spencer, was Jacquelyn Kennedy's personal priest.

The next year, I was a senior in high school. I auditioned to be Rose Princess — the annual Rose Festival and Parade are a big deal in Portland, Oregon — but I didn't get past the first level. I was still too tall, and added to that I was pimply, and not voluptuous.

Interestingly enough, twenty years later, I met an absolutely gorgeous woman, who made it all the way to first runner up for Rose Queen. All those years later, she still broke down and cried at the memory of her mother's cruel comment about her loss. Any sadness I had felt about my rejection had long since vanished. It was about that time that I realized that even the kids we all thought sailed through high school unscathed, carried their own scars.

Where did you go to high school?

_____

Who were your favorite friends?

1. _____
2. _____
3. _____
4. _____
5. _____

Who were your favorite teachers?

_____

What were your favorite subjects?

_____

What were your favorite activities?

1. _____
2. _____
3. _____
4. _____
5. _____

Who were your first loves?

_____

_____

What are your best high school memories?

1. _____
2. _____
3. _____
4. _____
5. _____

What is the story you tell yourself about that period of time?

_____

_____

_____

_____

_____

_____

_____

_____

_____

_____

_____

_____

_____

_____

_____

_____

_____

_____

How has this story affected you?

_____

_____

_____

_____

_____

_____

_____

_____

_____

_____

_____

_____

_____

_____

_____

Chapter Seven
COLLEGE YEARS
"The Rolling Stones, Porsches, and Hunks"

I attended a small liberal arts college for women in Pittsburgh, Pennsylvania. I went there intending to be a vocal performance major, but soon after I arrived, I switched to Political Science and History. I pretty much stopped singing for the next few years.

It was during my college years that beauty standards made a three hundred and sixty degree turn and for the first time in my life, tall and skinny was in!

I met great people at college. The Vietnam War was in full tilt during my college years, and the country was in turmoil. I did not know a single person who went to Vietnam until long after the war was over. I played hard, but I took care of business. I went to class. I studied hard, with one goal in mind: Graduating from college in four years. The theme song of my college years was, "We gotta get out of this place if it's the last thing we ever do." That pretty much summed it up for me, and everyone I knew.

My junior year, I went to New York City to the National Model United Nations at the old Statler Hilton Hotel. It was a blast: thousands of college students wandering the halls of the hotel day and night. I made some good friends there, and I met Bob McKenna, a law student. It was so loud in the party where I met him that I thought he said he went to Newark University Law School. In fact, he went to New York University Law School. He told me he'd graduated from Georgetown, and that he was from Pittsburgh, the same city where I went to college! We spent a nice evening together, and the next morning when we checked out of the hotel to go our separate ways, he said he'd call me.

A year passed. I was now a senior in college. I went back to the Model United Nations, and the first morning I was there, I saw him. My heart did a funny little flip, and I knew he might be the one. Now, I have to confess that I hadn't thought much about him in that year. There were lots of other guys, and he hadn't called me. I had some boyfriends from Princeton and Penn (The University of Pennsylvania) and they were there. I don't mean romantic boyfriends, but really good friends who were guys. It was three days of one long party. I was on the go the whole time.

Finally, on the last day of the conference, a group of us were sitting in a room doing some wrap-up work when Bob walked into the room. I was immediately aware of him. He sat quietly until the meeting was over, and then, as I was about to walk out of the room, he approached me and asked if I'd like to have a drink with him. That was it. I call it "love at first sight the second time around." We sat for hours talking.

He told me that he'd been in his hotel room with his best friend, Bob Mannix. He was debating whether he should take a nap or go try to find me. "Bobbi or nap?" he was asking himself. Thankfully, I won out over the nap. He also told me afterwards that he'd been calling my hotel room several times a day, trying to ask me out, but I was never in. "Why would I be sitting in my hotel room," I asked him, "When I could be out partying?"

~ ~ ~

Who were your best friends during the years between the ages of 18-22?

_____

_____

Who were your boyfriends or girlfriends?

_____

_____

If you went to college, where did you go?

_____

Who were your favorite professors?

_____

What were your favorite subjects?

_____

What are your most vivid memories of these years?

1. _____

_____

_____

_____

_____

_____

_____

_____

_____

_____

2. _____

_____

_____

_____

_____

_____

_____

_____

_____

3. _____

_____

_____

_____

_____

_____

_____

_____

4. _____

_____

_____

_____

_____

_____

_____

_____

_____

_____

5. _____

_____

_____

_____

_____

_____

_____

_____

_____

What is the story you tell yourself about this period of time?

_____

_____

_____

_____

_____

_____

_____

_____

_____

_____

_____

_____

_____

_____

_____

_____

Chapter Eight

REAL LOVE

"The Village Voice, a Hot Plate, and Star Trek Reruns"

Real love is what most of us seek and what we all yearn for. Some of us are lucky, and find people worthy of us and our dreams — people who make us better, and who grow with us over a lifetime.

I returned to college, and Bob and I kept in loose touch, mostly through letters. There wasn't any Internet or cell phones, and Long Distance phone calls were expensive. I wondered whether I would see him again, and then an opportunity presented itself. Skimmer Weekend at Penn. I traveled to Philadelphia from Pittsburgh, and he came down from New York City.

We stayed in an old house my Penn buddies were renting. Bob and I had a great time, but I still wasn't sure whether he was the real deal or not. He seemed sweet and sincere, but let's face it, with men sometimes, it's hard to tell. He was very different from most guys I'd dated. He'd been in ROTC at Georgetown, and he had a four and a half year commitment to the Army after he finished law school. He was in a special program that enabled him to go to law school, and then go on active duty as an officer in JAG: the Judge Advocate General's Corps.

Everyone else I knew had deferments and was thoroughly against the war. Bob felt it would be dishonorable to try to avoid military service since someone would have to go in his place — someone who was less privileged than he was.

I went back to college, finished up my last semester and graduated! FREEDOM! I went to New York to spend a couple of days with Bob at his dorm room at NYU in Greenwich Village.

It was that early time in any relationship where you and the other person confess your likes and dislikes. Like whether "Casablanca" is or isn't your all time favorite movie. In my case, it isn't because "Bringing Up Baby" with Katherine Hepburn and Cary Grant is. (In his case it's probably a "Three Stooges" or "Jackie Chan" movie. I remember when he accidentally taped over six hours of Three Stooges movies and was nearly reduced to tears.)

Anyway, I remarked that I pretty much disliked all sports. He laughed and replied, "And now you're going to marry a jock."

The words hung in the air. I could see them. I could hear them ringing in the silence. Later, when I would tell him how much the words surprised me, he told me that they were as much of a shock to him as to me. Since neither of us was ready to deal with what those words might mean, we acted as though they hadn't been said.

He went off to Fort Dix in New Jersey (on active duty for the summer), and I went to Washington, DC where I worked in the Department of Education.

I traveled to New Jersey to spend weekends with him, and he came to DC to spend time with me. We watched the moon landing together, listened to Crosby Stills and Nash and Bob Dylan albums and sweated in my "un-air conditioned" townhouse near Dupont Circle.

At the end of the summer, Bob returned to law school in New York's Greenwich Village. I packed my bags and moved to New York. I got a job in the Mayor's Office, and Bob and I grew closer.

I made it clear that I was not going to hang around indefinitely: it was marriage or "Sayonara, baby."

The Saturday before Christmas, we went with our friend, Bob Mannix, to his parents' home in Brooklyn. His mother was a great cook, and everyone drank too much. Mannix decided to stay the night in Brooklyn, and Bob and I headed for the subway back to Manhattan. We fell asleep, and almost slept past our stop.

We ended up at an all night deli because Bob wanted to buy some beer to take home. Obviously, he needed more alcohol! He also bought a Village Voice (newspaper), which was to figure prominently in our future. As we walked back to Bob's residence hall, we began to argue about something now long forgotten. Let's just say: "Words were spoken in anger."

Bob finally became so exasperated with me (obviously unjustifiably so) that he said, "If you don't stop that right now, I'm going to throw my Village Voice on the sidewalk." (I have omitted any cursing he may, or may not, have indulged in.)

I must not have stopped doing whatever it was that he wanted me to stop doing because the next thing I knew he threw his Village Voice on the sidewalk. (He would show me!)

I told him to pick up the paper. He refused and we walked back to his room still arguing. Once we got there, I decided to stay the night. I also announced that time was running out. If we didn't get married soon, I would take a job in Switzerland.

As we fell asleep, I said, "I'm going to Geneva in March unless we get married. What do you think about that?"

Bob's reply was: "I was thinking we should get married over Christmas break so we can get a dorm room for married couples when the new semester starts in January."

(Is this guy romantic or what? He wants to get married over Christmas, not because he loves me, but so he can get a bigger apartment.) The law school dorm, which was a large apartment building on Washington Square, had a small number of efficiency apartments that were reserved for married students.

The next day, neither of us mentioned what he'd said about getting married. I was afraid to bring it up, because I didn't know if he really meant it. Maybe he'd had so much to drink the night before that he wouldn't even remember having said it.

(He of course remembers it a bit differently. When I was writing this, I asked him what time in the afternoon we finally discussed his "proposal," and he replied that it was first thing. "I woke up bold, ready to go," he said, with a laugh.)

We went through our usual Sunday routine: reading The Sunday New York Times, doing the puzzle, and watching football with law school friends who dropped by. It was late in the afternoon before I got up the courage to ask him: 1) if he remembered what he'd said, and 2) if he meant it.

"Yup," he said. "I have to marry you because you made me so mad that I threw my Village Voice on the sidewalk and left it there. If that's not true love, what is?"

That's how I came to be married with only a one-week engagement and no diamond engagement ring. Some of you may be wondering why I would be willing to forego a big wedding. It was simple. I'd noticed that big weddings appeared to create enormous stress for all involved. As far as I was concerned, the major point of having a wedding was to get married to the person you loved.

The idea of overlaying it with a social event that cost thousands of dollars and provided numerous opportunities for conflict and second thoughts was counterproductive to achieving that goal. I had long ago concluded that I was not sufficiently mature at twenty-two to weather the emotional storms a big wedding would be sure to unleash.

Monday morning, I went to work at the Mayor's Office, and told my boss that I was flying to Pittsburgh on Tuesday to get married.

"You'll need a blood test," he said.

On Monday afternoon Bob and I had our blood drawn in the palatial office of the Director of the Department of Health for New York City by the Director himself. (There was no time to make a regular doctor's appointment so my boss in the Mayor's Office pulled a few strings.)

We got on a plane and flew to Pittsburgh to spend the Christmas holidays with Bob's family. I'll never forget the moment when we told Bob's parents about his brilliant idea to get married over Christmas Break so we could get a married student's apartment. We were standing in the kitchen of his parents' home. Bob's father was making a martini when Bob said, "Bobbi and I have some news. We've decided to get married"

His father chuckled and said, "Yes, Mom and I've been kind of expecting that. When are you planning to have the wedding?"

"What are you doing this Saturday?" Bob asked.

His father spilled gin onto the kitchen countertop.

"Where?" he asked.

"How about here in the house?" Bob replied.

The next day Bob's mother spent hours on the telephone inviting family members and close friends to a Saturday wedding. I heard her say over and over, "No, she isn't." It was, after all, a sudden wedding.

I called my dad and told him about the wedding. I didn't really expect him to come — he hadn't even come to my college graduation.

The day after Christmas I bought what seemed to be the only suitable white dress in Pittsburgh. It was a short white chiffon dress with a satin bodice.

Thursday night, with the wedding looming on Saturday, it suddenly struck me that I would be marrying this fine fellow. ("Idiot" was actually closer to the word I was thinking.) Let's just say that I was having a mini panic attack. I mentioned my misgivings to his mother, who said, "Oh, no you don't! I've already called all my friends and relatives…you're getting married on Saturday afternoon, and that's final!"

On Saturday, Bob and I were married in the living room of his parents' home by a judge who lived down the street from his parents. His mother ordered me a red rose corsage, but I had no bouquet and no wedding cake. Still, I got what I most needed: marriage to a man who adored me.

Here are the details that stand out in my memory:
- The wedding taking place during an east coast blizzard. Our best man, Bob Mannix, was stuck in a bar at Kennedy Airport for ten hours. He arrived just in time for the wedding, but without one of his dress shoes. It had fallen out of his suitcase when he was rummaging around looking for a pack of cigarettes.
- Bob's ninety year old Grandma McKenna arriving wearing her platinum blond wig,
- Bob's mother marching into the family room to turn off the TV to get his two brothers to come into the living room for the wedding. We got married at halftime during the Minnesota Vikings-LA Rams football game.
- One of Bob's uncles remarking, as Bob's dad escorted me into the living room for the wedding ceremony, "I hope the ceremony's as short as the bride's dress."
- The bright red splotches on Bob's cheeks as he took his vows.
- The wonderful party Bob's Mom and Dad gave for us at the Pittsburgh Athletic Association.

Back at law school in New York, we graduated from watching Star Trek reruns while Bob Mannix cooked dinner on a hot plate on the floor of his room to watching Star Trek reruns while I cooked dinner on our condo-sized stove top. Our one-room apartment was so small that we had to push all the chairs and tables to one corner of the room so we could pull the Murphy bed down out of the wall at night.

~   ~   ~

Where and how did you meet your first real love?

_____

_____

_____

_____

_____

_____

_____

_____

_____

_____

What was he or she like?

_____

_____

_____

_____

_____

_____

_____

_____

_____

_____

When and how did you know it was true love?

_____

_____

_____

_____

_____

_____

_____

_____

_____

_____

_____

_____

_____

_____

_____

If You Married

Describe the proposal:

_____

_____

_____

_____

_____

_____

_____

_____

_____

Describe your engagement:

_____

_____

_____

_____

_____

_____

_____

_____

_____

Describe your wedding:

_____

_____

_____

_____

_____

_____

_____

_____

_____

_____

_____

_____

_____

_____

_____

_____

~   ~   ~

If you have had more than one true love or one wedding, turn to the notes section in the back of the book to write about others

Chapter Nine
THE HONEYMOON AND MARRIED LIFE
"Loose Change, Swiss Chocolate, and Austrian Beer"

Bob finished law school, passed the Bar Exam in Pennsylvania and then we were off to the Army Judge Advocate General's (JAG) Corps training in Charlottesville. No matter what you may have seen on TV, JAG lawyers do not fly airplanes and shoot guns. They write wills, handle divorces, Article 32's, Court Martials, and even the occasional murder trial.

It wasn't until the October following our December wedding that we had time to go on our honeymoon. We saved money all summer. We even cashed in Bob's coffee can that was filled with loose change to buy our plane tickets to Europe.

Armed with a book titled, "Europe On $5 A Day," we flew on Icelandic Airlines to Luxembourg where everyone pretended not to be able to understand my French. From there, we went to Zurich, Switzerland by train where we spent a day in the Museum. Then, because Bob was an opera buff who especially revered the operas of Wagner, we went to Lucerne to see Wagner's home on the lake. At that time, Bob was entirely devoted to classical music. It would be many years before he would embark on his rebellious heavy metal period.

I did learn one surprising thing about him on our honeymoon. He was a nervous traveler! He worried, fretted, and complained constantly.

When we were waiting in the train station for the train to arrive, he would say, "I know the train isn't coming. We must be in the wrong place. I know we've missed it."

As soon as we would see the train beginning to pull into the train station, he would say: "I know we won't get a seat on the train."

As soon as were seated on the train, he would begin to worry about our hotel accommodations. (Traveling through Europe on $5 a day did not allow one to make hotel reservations in advance.)

In fact, almost everything worked perfectly although we did get the very last room in Lugano, Switzerland because we arrived during the wine festival.

Of course, as soon as we got a hotel room, he began to worry about the next train. We ate fabulous food everywhere we went. Bob taught me all the German he felt was really necessary. In the event that he was in the restroom when the waiter came, I was to say: "Zwei bier, bitte." (Two beers, please.) He proved himself a real hero when we were in Lugano, and he went out into the night to get me some Swiss chocolate while I soaked in a bubble bath.

We had a wonderful, magical, very sweet and romantic time, and again, I felt that doing the unconventional thing and taking our honeymoon months after our wedding worked in our favor.

Back in the USA, Bob's dad arranged for us to lease a dandelion-yellow sedan. We packed up, and headed west for Fort Leavenworth, Kansas where Bob's active duty military career was to begin in earnest. We went from Greenwich Village in New York City where the antiwar sentiment was at its height to an Army Post in the heartland of America where there wasn't even an echo of the outcry. As we drove onto the post, I sensed that I was entering another world.

If you went on a honeymoon, where did you go and when:

_____

Write down your five best memories of your honeymoon:

1. _____

_____

_____

_____

_____

2. _____

_____

_____

_____

_____

3. _____

_____

_____

_____

_____

4. _____

_____

_____

_____

_____

5. _____

_____

_____

_____

_____

~   ~   ~

If you had more than one honeymoon, turn to the note-
book in the back of the book and use the additional pages to
record your memories.

Chapter Ten
PREGNANCY AND MOTHERHOOD: "MOO MOO"
"Can't We Wait Until Tomorrow Morning To Go To The Hospital?"

Since I was on an Army Post in Kansas, and it would be several years before I would return to the East Coast and go to graduate school, my thoughts turned to babies. I read everything I could get my hands on dealing with the subject of pregnancy and childbirth.

Motherhood was something that I had a deep longing for. One nice thing about the Army was that it provided free medical care for military dependents at that time. My total cost for delivering my first child in a Army Hospital was $5.25 to cover the expense of the meals I ate.

I got pregnant after only a few months of trying. Around the end of the six month of my pregnancy, Bob's commanding officer told him that he would be getting a "Short Tour" assignment, which meant overseas: Vietnam, Korea, or Germany.

Since Vietnam was an active war zone, I wouldn't be able to accompany him there, which made it a very unappealing choice. But, because his "orders" hadn't yet been issued, he still had the option of volunteering to go to one of the other "short tour" destinations.

Bob called the Pentagon and asked the Major in charge of "Short Tour" assignments if he could volunteer to go to Germany where I could accompany him.

The Major responded: "Nice try, Captain, but no cigar. Try again."

"I volunteer to go to Korea, Sir," Bob said, picturing a clerk typist's hands poised over the keys of the old manual typewriter in the deep recesses of the Pentagon.

"Done!" the Major replied.

That's how close we came to being separated for a year instead of going to Korea as a family. The JAG Corps also deferred the actual deployment to Korea until after the birth of our baby. We were very, very lucky all around!

The third of February was a bitterly cold night that year in Kansas. When the Obstetrician on staff left for the day, he told the head nurse not to call him to deliver any babies that night.

Bob and I had taken La Maze Training for natural childbirth, and one of the major warnings we'd received was "Don't go to the hospital too soon! They'll just send you home." Several women I knew had gone to the hospital with false labor (Braxton Hicks contractions) and had been subjected to scornful derision from the hospital staff. I was determined not to suffer the same humiliation!

I'd been having Braxton Hicks contractions for three months, and they'd been growing progressively stronger. Nothing seemed that different on February 3rd. Strong contractions, but not much stronger than the ones I'd been having. I made up my mind that I would wait until my water broke before going to the hospital. About three in the morning, I got up to go the bathroom and my water broke. I woke Bob up, or tried to wake him up.

"Sweetheart," I said, "My water broke. We have to go the hospital to have the baby."

"Can't we wait and go in the morning," he mumbled.

I shook him. "No," I said, "we have to go now!"

Then, like any sensible woman, I got dressed, curled my eye-lashes, applied mascara and eye shadow, and then — and only then — did I get into our dandelion yellow sedan for the drive to the hospital. (I had my priorities straight, don't you think?)

As soon as I arrived at the hospital, I began doing my La Maze breathing. The nurse told me to knock it off.

"You're not nearly ready to be doing that," she said. Then, she took a look "down south" and sprinted for the telephone. Bob and I could hear her screaming for the doctor, who barely beat Baby McKenna to the hospital.

The delivery room had mirrors on the ceiling so I got to see my beautiful son come into the world. He was all golden and fuzzy. In my humble opinion, he was the most beautiful baby I'd ever seen. I held him in my arms and watched him breath. When we got him back home, I put him in our three hundred year old pine cradle right next to my side of the bed, and I watched him sleep. I was nursing, and he ate for an hour and a half — every three hours — which pretty much meant that I never slept.

We wanted to give him a distinctive name, and so we named him "Jason," which was a rather rare name in those days. Of course, millions of other parents thought the exact same thing at the exact same moment, and so he became one of millions of "Jasons."

We tried to avoid conformity by calling him "Jaimy," which was a boy's name at that time, and also rather rare. Well, wouldn't you know that when he was in Kindergarten, Hollywood would put on a TV show called the Bionic Woman, and the name of Bionic Woman was — "Jamie" Summers. That did it for Jaimy. He refused to go by a girl's name, and so he joined the ranks of the "Jasons." (Within our family circle, he has sometimes been called "Moo-Moo," after his favorite stuffed toy — a yellow cow that went "Moo"— that he had when he was a toddler.)

When Jason was five months old, Bob went to Korea and a week later, Jason and I went to join him. We flew from Pittsburgh to LA, where we stayed one night, and then to Hawaii and Tokyo, where we had to stay overnight in an airport hotel.

The next morning we flew to Seoul, Korea. When I got off the plane, I could smell the Kimchi. (This is fermented Korean cabbage or cucumber concoction with red peppers that is the staple of the Korean diet. It has — to put it mildly — a strong aroma.)

Now, most husbands would have rushed forward to welcome their wife and child, but I didn't see Bob at first because he was standing in the back of the crowd talking to someone! When I finally got his attention, he told me that he'd found a beautiful Korean home for us to live in.

We took the train to Taegu, the city south of Seoul where we would be living. We passed mile after mile of bright green rice paddies with people working in the paddies. In the city of Taegu, the streets were jammed with cyclists wearing black suits.

I, of course, was looking forward to seeing the beautiful house Bob had found for us. You can imagine my surprise when I discovered that it was not only in the back yard of a Korean doctor's house, but there were — and I am not kidding — WILD DOGS LIVING IN IT!

There I am, standing in a foreign country, which smells like fermented cabbage, all 110 lbs of me holding my precious baby, and this lunatic I have married actually expects me and my baby to live in a house that is already occupied by WILD DOGS!

I told him as forcefully as possible that we would not be living in the "WILD DOG" house. This was the first and last time Bob was ever delegated to make any real estate decisions for our family.

We did eventually find a nice Korean house to live in. It had sliding, etched-glass doors and a courtyard with a fishpond. It even had running water and a flush toilet — although the toilet was in a small building on the otherside of the yard. The late night dash across the graveled courtyard was challenging.

The floors of the house were made of shellacked paper, and the floors were heated by burning huge charcoal briquettes under the house. Only the floors got warm. The air in the house stayed as cold as the air outside. Since the floors were made of paper, we couldn't wear shoes inside the house. We slept on the floor on a "Yo," which was a THIN foam mattress. To get hot water for a shower, we had to fill the bathtub with cold water, put a wooden lid on it and then light another charcoal briquette which would gradually heat the bathtub full of water overnight. The shower was created by standing on the floor of the small bathroom, and pouring buckets of water over ourselves.

I got pregnant again almost right away, but the medical clinic told me I wasn't pregnant. It took me insisting on a new pregnancy test during the second month of my pregnancy to prove it.

Korea at that time was very different from the United States. Everywhere I went, crowds of people would follow me, fascinated by my long blond hair, blue eyes, "Jackie O' sunglasses" and "hot pants." They especially loved to rub Jason's head. He was a typical blond, bald baby, and they thought he was some kind of Buddha manifestation.

On Christmas Day, when Jason was ten months old, he walked a mile through downtown Taegu with his father. He was learning to speak English and Korean at the same time. He was always very smart and by the time he was fourteen months old, he knew twenty words in each language. He would use the languages appropriately: Korean words for our Korean baby sitter and English words for me.

Jason was always one of the smartest boys in school, and he has a clever and nimble mind. He's tall and slim like the Franklin family. When we lived in Washington, DC, he attended the National Cathedral Elementary School and Saint Albans School. He sang in the Cathedral Choir in Bethlehem Chapel where Supreme Court Justice Sandra Day O'Connor was an usher. He ran track at Saint Albans under Coach Grant, and many days when he was running, he shared the track with Vice President George Bush who would run while Secret Service agents sat watch at a picnic table. Jason swears that the agents had UZI's at the ready.

When he was in the 4th grade at Saint Alban's, Jason came with his brother, Spencer, and me to the Kennedy Center. I was singing in Leonard Bernstein's MASS, and Lennie had asked me and a few others to bring our sons in to audition for the show. Jason was wearing his Saint Alban's blazer and tie, sitting in a folding chair doing his homework. The casting director approached him and asked him to come to the piano so he could audition.

"Oh, no," he said. "I can't be in the show. I have too much school work."

He later told me that when he was in college, he sometimes woke up in the middle of the night, and relived the moment that he had turned down an opportunity to be in a Leonard Bernstein show BECAUSE HE HAD TOO MUCH HOMEWORK! Argh!

In high school, he played basketball and football, and is now a fifth degree black belt in Taekwondo. Also, during high school, Jason and his friends came to our house for lunch every day. One of my most vivid memories is of driving into my garage and seeing A BOY I HAD NEVER LAID EYES ON BEFORE, getting a frozen pizza out of MY freezer to cook in MY oven.

Every Saturday night, we had "sit down" dinners for any teenagers who wanted to come. My husband, Bob, would shop and cook for these dinners, and they took a huge bite out of our budget. But, both Bob and I always felt that we would rather have a house full of teenagers than not to know where our own kids were.   One of Jason's best friends was Matt Stone, the co-creator of South Park, who spent a lot of time at our house.   Matt was always very creative, and Jason predicted that he would be a huge success.

Jason is a graduate of The University of Colorado.   He has always been a wonderful son and big brother.   My wish for him is that he always knows how much he is treasured and loved by his father and me, and that he finds his true purpose and passion in life.

~   ~   ~

When and where was your first child born?

_____

_____

Write the story of your child's birth, giving as many details as possible:

_____

_____

_____

_____

_____

_____

Write down your first child's first words

_____

_____

_____

_____

Where and when did your first child walk?

_____

_____

_____

What are your five happiest memories of your child?

1. _____
2. _____
3. _____
4. _____
5. _____

What have been your child's greatest successes?

1. _____
2. _____
3. _____
4. _____
5. _____

Write three stories about your first child's infancy?

1. _____
_____
_____
_____
_____

2. _____
_____
_____
_____
_____

3. _____
_____
_____
_____
_____

Write three stories about his or her preschool years:

1. _____
_____
_____
_____

2. _____
_____

_____

_____

_____

3. _____

_____

_____

_____

Write three stories about your child's elementary school years (K-5ᵗʰ Grade):

1. _____

_____

_____

_____

_____

2. _____

_____

_____

_____

_____

3. _____

_____

_____

_____

_____

Write three stories about your child's middle school years (6th, 7th, 8th Grade):

1. _____
_____
_____
_____
_____

2. _____
_____
_____
_____
_____

3. _____
_____
_____
_____
_____

Write three stories about your child's high school years:

1. _____
_____
_____
_____

2. _____

_____

_____

_____

_____

3. _____

_____

_____

_____

_____

What are the stories that you tell yourself and others about your child?

_____

_____

_____

_____

_____

_____

_____

_____

_____

_____

_____

_____

_____

_____

_____

What are the "formative" stories you have told your child about him or herself?

_____

_____

_____

_____

_____

_____

_____

_____

_____

_____

_____

_____

_____

_____

_____

_____

_____

_____

How do you think these stories have affected you?

_____

_____

_____

_____

_____

_____

_____

_____

_____

_____

_____

_____

_____

_____

_____

_____

How do you think these stories have affected your child?

_____

_____

_____

_____

_____

_____

_____

_____

_____

_____

_____

_____

_____

_____

_____

What are your hopes and wishes for your child in the years ahead?

_____

_____

_____

_____

_____

What are your child's dreams?

_____

_____

_____

_____

_____

What can you do to support those dreams?

_____

_____

_____

_____

_____

Chapter Eleven
NEW BABY MAKES FOUR
"Benny Bunson or Bunny Benson?"
"Korea, Kimchi, And Taking A Chopper To The Hospital"

The doctors told me that my second baby, who was to be Spencer, would be born on March 31. The military practice at that time was to send pregnant women on the train from Taegu to the 121st Evacuation Hospital in Seoul. (The 121st EVAC Hospital is where they sent the soldiers on the TV Show MASH after "Hawkeye" patched them up.)

Right before my due date, a woman had given birth on the train because of this policy, and since my first labor had been so short, Bob got permission for us to go to Seoul the day before, and to go by helicopter and not the train. (We could only stay there a couple of days so if the baby had come late, I'm not sure what would have happened.) Anyway, that's how I ended up going to the 121st EVAC Hospital in Seoul, Korea in a helicopter to have my baby.

Again, I was concerned about not going to the hospital too soon. The night that my second child was born, Bob and I went out dancing until he began to suspect that I was in labor. He tricked me into going to the hospital by saying we should just "let them know" that I was in Seoul.

I said, "Okay, but I'm not taking my suitcase."

Bob humored me, pretty sure that I was in labor and that he

would have to make an extra trip back to the place we were staying to get my suitcase. He was right. Shortly after I got to the hospital, Spencer was born.

Two days later, the three of us took the train back to Taegu. I still remember the Korean businessmen on the train staring at the skinny blond woman and her blond baby. We had another month in Korea before we could return to the U.S. Just before we were to leave, the Presbyterian missionaries who we had rented our house from, asked us if we would adopt a little eighteen month old baby that they were caring for in the hospital.

I was only twenty-six. We had barely enough money to live on. We already had a fifteen month old and a one month old, and I was planning to go to graduate school fulltime. I told them that I couldn't do it then, but I made a promise to myself that I would adopt a Korean baby sometime in the future.

We said goodbye to all our Korean friends and left for the USA. We went from Taegu to Seoul by bus, and then we flew via Japan, Anchorage and Chicago to Pittsburgh where Bob's parents lived.

After a year in Korea, the people in Chicago looked very, very pale to me. I suffered as much culture shock — if not more — coming back from Korea than I had going from the USA to Korea. There were so many cars and so many people, and the department stores were so huge and filled with so many things!

I was "back in the world," as the Vietnam Vets of the time put it, and I was ready to go to graduate school and begin my real life. We had Spencer's baptism in Copley Crypt at Georgetown University with Father Richard McSorley officiating, and then we had a great Christening Party afterwards. That first summer back in the United States with a fifteen-month old toddler and a one-month old baby boy was a challenge. If I found one hour a day when I could even sit down and read a book, it was a miracle. My biggest fear and challenge was being able to find a babysitter I could trust my children with so I could start graduate school in the fall. At one point, I told Bob I couldn't go to grad school because I was afraid to leave the boys. He told me that I was being ridiculous, and then, at the last minute, I found someone wonderful.

The two little boys were towheads, just like Bob and I had been. They were only fourteen months apart and looked so much alike that people always asked me if they were twins. Their personalities, however, were quite different. Jason jabbered words the minute he could form them in his mouth. Spencer waited until he could speak in a complete sentence. One day, as we were driving down I-95 going from Alexandria into the District of Columbia, I heard Spencer say in absolutely perfect diction: "The sun is shining in my eyes."

The next day he was playing with his Mr. Potato Head toy. He kept trying to put Mr. Potato Head's glasses on himself. Bob was afraid he would poke himself in the eye, and so he said, "Spencer, don't put Mr. Potato Head's glasses on!" Apparently, Spencer didn't stop, because the next thing I knew, he was tugging on my skirt and saying: "Daddy took 'Tato Head's glasses away from me."

While Jason loved to run everywhere pell-mell, Spencer was more cautious. He thought being carried was preferable to walking anywhere. While Jason learned to ride a bike when he was six by just getting on and falling down a dozen or more times, Spencer waited until he could do it perfectly.

He was also little "Mr. Me-Too." Whenever Bob would say anything to Jason, Spencer would say, "Me, Too, Daddy? Me, Too?" It was when the boys were in nursery school that Jason became "Moo-Moo." Everyday, Spencer would go out to the playground to find Jason. One day he came home and told me, "I went to the playground, but I couldn't find my Jaimy Moo-Moo, and so I sat down."

Spencer also loved to play what he called "big life," which was make-believe. (Jason preferred to play with action figures which was called "little life.") When Spencer was about four years old, he created two alter egos: Bunny Benson, who was angelic, and Benny Bunson, who was his "evil" twin. Bob and I got into the habit of asking him if he was "Bunny Benson" or "Benny Bunson" so we would know what to expect at any given moment.

Meanwhile, I was in graduate school at the Institute for Sino-Soviet Studies at George Washington University. I'll never forget the first day I left the boys, who were twenty months and five months old, in Alexandria. I got on a bus and went into DC. It was the first time in months that I had been out of my "baby puke" clothes. All dressed up, walking down "H" Street, I remember being shocked that all the people looked at me and thought I was a real person. (Probably, only Mommies who have spent a lot of time home with young children will understand this comment.)

Spencer sang in the Cathedral Choir in Bethlehem Chapel. He played tennis, and studied piano. Every summer, Spencer and Jason attended the Saint Alban's Summer Day Camp because I was working. There were always little plays that the campers put on, and Bob and I would take off from work to go see the boys in their plays. I remember one summer in particular. Jason's play came first. He was super as always, but when Spencer who had always been a little shy, came out onto the stage and belted out a solo, we were stunned. He was the head goblin, and his song went like this: "Look out for us, we are the goblins of the mountain." That's all I remember.

A few weeks later I took the boys to the Kennedy Center to see the Broadway Show "Annie," which was touring. Both the run of Leonard Bernstein's MASS to celebrate the Kennedy Center's tenth anniversary. A few days into rehearsals, Bernstein asked some of the singers, myself included, to bring our children in to audition for the small children's choir which appears in the play.

Spencer auditioned and was selected to be in the show. He said something like this to me: "You know when we saw 'Annie' last month, I never dreamed that only a month later, I would be singing and dancing on the same stage."

He was the youngest and smallest one, and he stood right in the center front of the children's choir. It was broadcast on TV worldwide and so we have the videotape of one of the performances. We did eight shows a week for three and a half weeks.

It was a great bonding experience for Spencer and me. On Friday night, we would do one show. Then, we would do two more on Saturday — a matinee and an evening show — with two more on Sunday. Since there really wasn't enough time to go home and get back in time, we would just stay at the Kennedy Center all day. We would hang out in the dressing rooms, and the performers' canteen. We got to know the whole cast, including Leonard Bernstein's daughter, very well.

Spencer also sang in "Christmas in Washington," an annual TV Special hosted by Andy Williams when Ronald Reagan was president. Spencer came home from one taping and said, "You know a lot of people might be excited about seeing the President and singing on TV, but I'm getting kind of bored with it."

He played football at Saint Alban's, and he was captain of the Eighth Grade team. The summer after that we moved to Colorado where he played football for a couple of years until he hurt his knee.

In high school in Colorado, Spencer put together his own heavy metal band, which rehearsed at our house. He had waist long blond hair, and he was a very talented guitarist. My Dad called him "Axel" for Axel Rose. Spencer took his music very seriously — so seriously that he ended up firing all the other members of the band — who he felt were slacking off. One of the band members he fired was his brother Jason.

Spencer graduated from Colorado State University, and is now a Captain in the United States Air Force. He is also fluent in Arabic.

Spencer is a wonderful son and brother. We wish for him all the blessings we have received and more!

✦　　✦　　✦

When and where was your second child born?

_____

_____

Write the story of your child's birth, giving as many details as possible:

_____

_____

_____

_____

_____

_____

_____

_____

_____

_____

_____

_____

_____

_____

_____

_____

_____

_____

Write down your second child's first words:

_____

_____

_____

_____

Where and when did your second child walk?

_____

_____

_____

_____

_____

_____

What are your five happiest memories of your child?

1. _____
2. _____
3. _____
4. _____
5. _____

What have been your child's greatest successes?

1. _____
2. _____
3. _____
4. _____
5. _____

Write three stories about your second child's infancy?

1. _____

_____

_____

_____

_____

2. _____
_____
_____
_____
_____

3. _____
_____
_____
_____
_____

Write three stories about his or her preschool years:

1. _____
_____
_____
_____
_____

2. _____
_____
_____
_____
_____

3. _____
_____
_____

_____

_____

Write three stories about your child's elementary school years (K-5th Grade):

1. _____

_____

_____

_____

_____

2. _____

_____

_____

_____

_____

3. _____

_____

_____

_____

_____

Write three stories about your child's middle school years (6th, 7th, 8th Grade):

1. _____

_____

_____

_____

_____

2. _____

_____

_____

_____

_____

3. _____

_____

_____

_____

_____

Write three stories about your child's high school years:

1. _____

_____

_____

_____

2. _____

_____

_____

_____

3. _____

_____

_____

_____

_____

What are the stories that you tell yourself and others about your child?

_____

_____

_____

_____

_____

_____

_____

_____

_____

_____

_____

_____

_____

_____

_____

_____

_____

_____

_____

_____

What are the "formative" stories you have told your child about him or herself?

_____

_____

_____

_____

_____

_____

_____

_____

_____

_____

_____

_____

_____

_____

_____

_____

_____

_____

_____

_____

_____

How do you think these stories have affected you?

_____

_____

_____

_____

_____

_____

_____

_____

_____

How do you think these stories have affected your child?

_____

_____

_____

_____

_____

_____

_____

_____

_____

What are your hopes and wishes for your child in the years ahead?

_____

_____

_____

_____

_____

What are your child's dreams?

_____

_____

_____

_____

_____

What can you do to support those dreams?

_____

_____

_____

_____

_____

_____

_____

_____

_____

_____

_____

_____

_____

_____

_____

_____

_____

_____

_____

_____

_____

_____

_____

_____

_____

_____

Chapter Twelve
STARTING MY CAREER AND GETTING FIRED!
"Foggy Bottom, Capitol Hill, and Sleepy Hollow"

I already had two children and was twenty-six when I enrolled in graduate school at George Washington University, located in the area of Washington, DC known as "Foggy Bottom." I had two teaching fellowships: one from the Institute for Sino-Soviet Relations and the other from the History Department.

It was a challenging period of my life, to say the least: three years of spending every night studying after I put the boys to bed. I got to meet scholars from all over the world, and top policy makers in the U.S. Government. Finally, I passed my doctoral comps, and we moved from Alexandria, Virginia into the District of Columbia.

We rented a townhouse on Quebec Street, within walking distance of the National Cathedral so the boys could go to the Cathedral Elementary School. It took me a few months, but I finally got a job on Capitol Hill in a Congressman's Office. It was an amazing experience.

What I discovered was that very young people — only in their twenties in some cases — are writing many of the laws we live by. Senators and Representatives are so busy that they must rely on their office and committee staffs. The second week I was there, I was offered a job in the Defense Intelligence Agency. It would not only mean more money, I was also told that there would be a promotion in a year. In addition, the work would be directly in my field of interest: China. In the Congressman's Office, I was a legislative correspondent in the area of international relations, which meant that I answered letters to the Congressman that dealt with foreign policy issues. I also thought that my country would benefit from my service.

I accepted the job with DIA, and was immediately sent to the Defense Intelligence School in Anacostia. I had to get up at 4 o'clock in the morning and take two buses to get there from Northwest DC. I did well in the class and received the Outstanding Briefer's Award. I was also named a Distinguished Graduate of the Defense Intelligence School.

During the time I was at the Defense Intelligence School, Edward Teller, the famous scientist paid a visit to the school. The military officers in charge of the school were very excited about his coming. Our class was divided up into sub groups to develop threat assessments on various potential trouble spots in the world. I believe that my group was assigned to study Panama.

As we discussed all the factors at play there, most of the people in my group thought that everything would be fine. I presented the other point of view in our group discussion, but I was prepared to go with the majority for our presentation. The Major who was the instructor for this class thought that Teller would like it, if I presented a dissenting point of view. He asked me to do that.

First, the spokeswoman for our group presented the group assessment, and then I presented the other point of view. Teller loved it. And at the end of the day, before he left, he complimented us on my dissent because he thought one of the greatest weaknesses of American intelligence gathering and reporting was the push for conformity at the expense of truthfulness.

After I graduated from the Defense Intelligence School, I was assigned to the China Division of DIA, which was at Arlington Hall Station, an old Army Post in Northern Virginia. It was like going back in time. Within the Intelligence Community at that time, DIA at Arlington Hall Station was called "Sleepy Hollow."

I had been hired because President Carter's Administration was trying to bring more women into parts of the federal government that had traditionally been mostly male. As soon as I got to my assignment, I realized that many staff members of DIA did not appreciate President Carter's policies promoting equal employment opportunity for women. I shared an office with three men who had worked together for a long time. All three had served in the military, as had most of the civilian intelligence analysts at that time.

I worked hard as always, and did well. This can be a big mistake, which you know if you've ever seen the TV Show "Survivor." The best strategy for surviving in any bureaucracy is the same as it is on the TV Island: Don't stick your head up. Don't excel. And, fly under the radar as long as possible.

My boss, who was a Lieutenant Colonel, was impressed with my work ethic and the quality of the analysis I produced. As a consequence, he decided to take a plum assignment away from one of the men I worked with, and he gave it to me. You know what happened next, don't you?

Sure you do, the man who lost the assignment organized the rest of the men in the unit. They went to the boss and complained about me. I was disrupting the work environment. I found this out at my eleven-month evaluation when the Lieutenant Colonel showed me my personnel evaluation form in which he had given me almost all "Superior" ratings. He had also written: "Mrs. McKenna represents the new blood that DIA needs."

There was however one area where I did not receive an outstanding evaluation. It was getting along with others. I could have (and should have) just bided my time. In one month, I would pass the one-year probationary period, and I would have come under Civil Service regulations, which would have given me more legal rights.

My husband, Bob, who was practicing Equal Employment Opportunity law at the time, told me that I could not let the bad evaluation stand. I had to complain. In order to do that, I had to go over the head of my supervisor to the top man in the Division, a Navy Captain. The Captain was disturbed by what I told him. He said it sounded like he had "a can of worms" on his hands, and he even told me that it wasn't for nothing that Arlington Hall was known as "Sleepy Hollow." He told me he would order an investigation. Then, he went on vacation, expecting to have the written report of the investigation on his desk when he returned. In the meantime, the Lieutenant Colonel, who was my immediate supervisor, and the Colonel who was his supervisor fired me for "going outside the chain of command."

The chain of command is sacrosanct in many parts of the government. According to this principle if you work for a government agency and you report a threat to your boss — let's say something like Arab men taking flying lessons — and your boss does not find the threat credible, he or she can decline to pass the threat up the chain of command, and that's the end of it.

If you violate the chain of command by going over your boss's head to report the threat, you face demotion or firing. Does this sound familiar?

To support their case, they also cited the fact that I was so disagreeable that I refused to accept the assessment of my working group at the Defense Intelligence School and had insisted on airing my dissent in front of our distinguished visitor Dr. Teller, much to everyone's shock and dismay. (As you can see, they got me good!)

The night of September 11, 2001, I told my husband, " You know good and well that there were people who knew enough about this to stop it. You also know that they told their superiors, and that they refused to pass it up the chain of command." My words have been proven true by the testimony of FBI officials who tried to pass on the warnings.

Anyway, to get back to my story, there I was: After all the years of hard work, I was fired in forty-eight hours. My only chance to save my career was to get someone higher up to intervene. One of Bob's law partners was able to get me a meeting with an Admiral who was one of the top men in DIA. I went to his office at the Pentagon, and made my case.

"How could it be," I asked him "that one week, I was one of the top people in my unit, and the next week I am fired?"

The Admiral interrupted me and said, "You're a brilliant woman Mrs. McKenna, but we don't need brilliant women in DIA."

That pretty much says it all. I include this story because I'm not the only one who has ever been fired from a job. It happens every day to hardworking people, and when it happens, it can be absolutely devastating.

In my case, the story I'd told myself — "If I work hard and always do my best, the word will give me its best." — that story was in tatters. I needed a new story if I was to go forward and not be undone by this event.

When I confided to a friend of mine, who was a graduate of West Point, about the depth of my grief over losing this job, he said this to me: "Something was stolen from you that you had worked very hard for."

That was a powerful description but it was only one element of the new story I was about to write for myself. First, I had to reduce "the factual elements" of the firing to lessons I could use in the future. I began to realize almost at once that being fired from DIA was the best thing that could have happened to me.

I might never have had the wisdom or the courage to quit that job. I would have stayed there for twenty or thirty years, and not been able to be present during many of the most important formative years in my children's life. Once I was home with them, I realized how much they needed me.

This is not meant as a criticism of anyone who works fulltime. As I already said, I didn't leave my job, my job left me. I also don't mean to imply that children who have two working parents don't turn out just as well, or better, than children who do have a parent at home. And let's not forget the fact that although we needed the money I earned, my salary was not the only source of income for our family.

That said, let's get back to the writing of my new story. (No, I didn't actually write it down although I probably would today. I just created it in my mind, and told it to myself.)

The first part of the process of writing my new story was to acknowledge that my being fired (which was meant to hurt me) had actually turned out to be a blessing. The second part of the process was to identify all the lessons I could learn from the experience. Here is a rough rundown of the lessons I derived from the story of why and how I was fired:

- Try not to take a job in a hostile work environment. (Now, of course, I didn't realize that DIA would be a hostile work environment, but I should have, which leads to the next lesson I learned.)
- Do as much research as possible before jumping into any situation. Know what you're getting into.
- When you work in a bureaucracy, or if you're on the TV Show "Survivor," keep your head down. Fly under the

radar as long as possible. Realize that promotions or "winning a challenge" can sometimes lead to disaster.

- If you have only a month until you get civil service protection, don't make any complaints about your boss no matter what your husband or wife tells you to do.
- Don't become financially and emotionally dependent on your job.
- Know that if you do your best work, there are people who will resent you. As I put it now, "if you don't want to be criticized or attacked, don't do anything.
- When people ask you to be frank in the workplace, don't do it! Keep your thoughts to yourself if you want to keep your job.
- Realize that other people are going to put their self-interest first. That's a fact. Try to find a way for everyone to win.
- Enjoy people, help them, and never say anything bad about anyone.
- Don't go along with the mob when they're out to hurt someone. Say the right thing, do the right thing, and if you suffer because of it, so be it!

List all the jobs you've held during your lifetime, and tell what you gained from each.

_____

_____

_____

_____

_____

_____

_____

_____

_____

_____

Have you ever been fired? If so, what are the lessons you learned from that experience?

_____

_____

_____

_____

_____

How do you feel about what you're doing now?

_____

_____

_____

_____

_____

If you could do anything, what would you like to be doing?

_____

_____

_____

_____

_____

What resources do you need in order to create your dream career?

_____

_____

_____

_____

_____

∽   ∽   ∽

Chapter Thirteen
ADOPTION "HILLY"
"At The Airport: This is Your Baby ~ We Love Her!"

For the next several years, I worked part time at the Alban Institute on the grounds of the National Cathedral. I also began singing again. I walked into Saint Albans Church on Wisconsin Avenue and auditioned for the church choir, thinking it was a garden-variety, neighborhood church choir. Instead, the director of the choir (which turned out to be a professional choir) was one of the most influential musicians in Washington, DC. In addition to the church choir, he had his own small ensemble, and a large concert choir, The Choral Arts Society, which performed regularly at the Kennedy Center.

During those years, I felt — like most American women — as though I were a performer in a three-ring circus. Perched on the high wire, juggling a husband, kids, a job, and singing in my "spare" time. This was a stressful time. These are the years when most marriages fail. Bob was trying to get his legal career established after the years in the military, and Washington, DC is a very expensive city to live in. Jason and Spencer were in private school, and my part-time job did not generate the income that would have come from the government job I'd lost.

It was at this time that I began to think about wanting to take Jason and Spencer to see my Dad, who hadn't seen them since his trip to DC years before. I hadn't been back to Portland because I was worried about how to deal with my mother. I bought plane tickets for the boys and me to go to Portland in June, and then I began to have misgivings about my mother.

How could I go there and not see her — she was, after all, my mother — but if I saw her, I knew she would try to pull me back into her chaotic world. Plus, I didn't really know what she might be capable of, or how violent she might be. I didn't want to expose my sons to her. I didn't want them to even have to know that people like her existed. I wanted to shelter them from what I had endured.

The end of March, just before Spencer's birthday, I got a call from my mother's aunt telling me that my mother had died from a drug overdose. I hadn't really realized until that moment just how deep my fear of her had been. I felt as though a dark shadow — that had been blotting out the sun — was suddenly gone! I took the boys to Portland to meet my dad, and from there, we all went to Longview so that they could become initiated into the "happy ways" of the Franklin Clan.

About the same I began thinking about the promise I'd made years before to adopt a baby girl from Korea. Bob and I'd been trying to have another baby ever since Spencer was about five years old, but I hadn't been able to get pregnant. We consulted doctors who told us that Bob's two hernia surgeries after Spencer was born were probably to blame.

After I got back from seeing my dad's family, I got out the phone book and started looking for an adoption agency. The first call I made was to Lutheran Family Services. The woman I talked to told me that they didn't handle adoptions, but she'd heard about a new adoption agency that was just starting up. She gave me the phone number, and then she told me that she was looking for a home for a Vietnamese teenager. "He's a senior in high school.

He just needs a home for one year," she said, "and you live near the high school he's enrolled in now."

She also told me that his name was Tuan Huyhn, and that he was an "unaccompanied minor" whose mother had used all the families' gold to pay for his passage by boat out of Vietnam. Tuan had been living with another family for three years, but the other family had not been able to come to terms with the fact that he wasn't living up to their expectations for him.

I told the woman at Lutheran Social Services that I would ask my husband. Bob was surprised.

"I thought you were calling about a baby girl," he said, "and now you tell me we're getting an 18 year old boy?"

"It's just for a year," I said. "He needs to finish high school."

"Where will he sleep?" Bob asked.

We were living in a fifteen hundred square foot, eighty year old house in Washington, DC. We were using all three bedrooms upstairs, but there was a fourth bedroom in the basement, which Bob used as an exercise room.

"Downstairs," I said.

"Where will I work out?" Bob asked.

"You could use the living room," I said.

He knew that I hated to have him work out in the living room because it always smelled like a gym for hours afterwards.

"Okay," he said. "Let's do it."

That's how Tuan came to live with us. He was a nice, pleasant, handsome young man. His father, who had been an officer in the South Vietnamese Army, was in a communist prison in Vietnam, and his mother and the rest of his family had been relocated to the countryside. Tuan told me that he had not wanted to leave Vietnam, but his mother had forced him to go. She said "Try to get to the USA. If not USA, Australia or Canada."

He had spent three years in a refugee camp in Indonesia. It

was, he said, the happiest time in his life. He played all day with other unaccompanied children, dove for abalone and waited for his number to be called. One day, he heard his number, and then, "USA."

Tuan was very gifted in math and did extremely well on his math SAT despite having — in my opinion — a very slim grasp of English. We liked him and he got along well with us. Now, I had an eighteen-year old boy who was almost a man to add to my two boys, who were almost ten and almost eleven.

I called the number of the adoption agency that might have Korean babies, and talked to Mr. Kim, the man in charge.

I made an appointment for Bob and me to meet with Mr. Kim and a social worker. Because it was a new agency, they had babies waiting for families instead of the other way around. It took two months for our "Home Study" to be completed, and then, we received a photo of our baby.

Her name was Jung Yoon Sook, and she was the most beautiful baby girl we'd ever seen. It was the end of October, and we would have to wait until three babies were ready to come. The agency would not allow us to go to Korea to get her.

It was a Saturday in December before we got any more news about our baby. It was an icy cold day, and our telephone wasn't working. I think there was ice on the phone line or something.

At two-thirty in the afternoon, the phone rang and the social worker said, "Mrs. McKenna, you're baby will be arriving Tuesday night at National Airport."

I hung up, and tried to call Bob, who was working at the office. THE PHONE DID NOT WORK! It only worked for that one phone call all day: the call that told us our baby girl was coming from Korea.

Tuesday night, we all went to National Airport: Bob, Jason, Spence, Tuan, and I. We waited a short time, with the three boys watching TV in the VIP lounge. Finally, we went to the gate, and then, the social worker went onto the plane and brought back our baby. She was six and half months old, and perfectly beautiful! We named her Hilary.

I held her in my arms and gave her a bottle, and she looked up into my eyes. I could see her bonding with me in that second. For the next two weeks, I couldn't put her down, or she would howl. She had been cared for by a foster mother and hadn't been in an orphanage. In Korea, a baby is strapped to its mother's back, and thus always in physical contact with its mother. I knew this because I'd lived in Korea.

The first night we took her home, Tuan showed her a spoonful of rice, and told her, "When you get older, you're going to really like rice."

Spencer and Jason adored her. When she started to talk, she called Spencer, "Bubby." He even began to refer to himself as Bubby as in "Hilly, give Bubby the priceless crystal heirloom right now!"

We had a toy poodle named Puffy, and Hilary ate his dog food once. For fourteen years after that, he always got really worried whenever she was near his food. He would growl and scamper to his dish.

Her favorite TV show was Punky Brewster, and she wore her hair the same way Punky did. Spencer and Jason took her to the park and she loved to swing. She would jump out of the swing and yell, "Punky Power!"

She called herself "a little ghoul" instead of "a little girl." When Spencer was at school, and I took her to the park, she would look around for him and then say "Bubby all gone."

She couldn't say "Hilary" so she called her self "EE-EE." She sometimes shortened it just to "EE," and she talked about herself in the third person, as in "EE hungry." "EE happy." "EE sad."

I remember vividly the day when she became an American citizen. We got a babysitter for Christopher (the new baby who you will learn about in the next chapter) and then Bob, Hilly, the big boys and I went down to the Federal Courthouse on Constitution Avenue. As soon as we got there, we knew something unusual was happening. There were Secret Service agents everywhere and bomb-sniffing dogs. Finally, we spotted Vice President George Bush and his wife Barbara coming into the courtroom. One of their longtime employees was also becoming an American citizen that day, too.

When Hilary was five, we moved to Colorado. She played the piano, and loved to swim. She was a great "butterfly" swimmer and then, she switched to back stroke in high school. She was an All American Swimmer.

She spent a lot of time with my family in Longview, and she loved to go to the beach. One summer, she and I drove down the Oregon Coast all the way to Newport. We went to Hawaii many times. Perhaps the most fun time for me was when we went for New Year's 2000 to Maui, and she and Christopher were swimming in the ocean at midnight. On New Year's Day, we saw dozens and dozens of humpback whales.

She was definitely Mommy's girl. When she was six and seven, I went one time a year to a church retreat in the Rockies. The second year I went, I told her I was going, and she said, "Again?"

Now she's in college in Colorado, and almost all grown up. She has given our family love and joy, and we wish for her a lifetime of love, joy, and happiness!

～   ～   ～

When and how did you first begin to think about adopting a child?

_____

_____

_____

_____

_____

_____

Describe the first steps in the adoption process:

_____

_____

_____

_____

_____

_____

When and how did you tell family and friends about your decision to adopt?

_____

_____

_____

_____

_____

_____

Describe the first time you saw your child's photo. (What happened and how did you feel?)

_____

_____

_____

_____

_____

When and where was your child born?

_____

_____

_____

Write as much as you know about your child's birth and birth parents:

_____

_____

_____

_____

_____

_____

_____

_____

_____

Describe when and how you saw your child and held him or her in your arms for the first time?

_____

_____

_____

_____

_____

If you had to travel to another country to get your baby, describe your trip:

_____

_____

_____

_____

_____

_____

_____

_____

_____

_____

_____

_____

Write down your child's first words:

_____

_____

_____

_____

_____

Where and when did your child walk?

_____

_____

_____

_____

_____

_____

_____

What are your five happiest memories of your child?

1. _____

2. _____

3. _____

4. _____

5. _____

What have been your child's greatest successes?

1. _____
2. _____
3. _____
4. _____
5. _____

If your child was still an infant when he or she came to live with you, write down three stories about your child's infancy?

1. _____
_____
_____
_____
_____

2. _____
_____
_____
_____
_____

3. _____
_____
_____
_____
_____

Write three stories about his or her preschool years:

1. _____

_____

_____

_____

_____

2. _____

_____

_____

_____

_____

3. _____

_____

_____

_____

Write three stories about your child's elementary school years (K-5th Grade):

1. _____

_____

_____

_____

2. _____

_____

_____

_____

_____

3. _____

_____

_____

_____

_____

What are the stories that you tell yourself and others about your child?

_____

_____

_____

_____

_____

_____

_____

_____

_____

_____

_____

_____

_____

_____

_____

_____

_____

What are the "formative" stories you have told your child about him or herself?

_____

_____

_____

_____

_____

_____

_____

_____

_____

_____

_____

_____

_____

_____

_____

_____

_____

_____

How do you think these stories have affected you?

_____

_____

_____

_____

_____

_____

_____

_____

How do you think these stories have affected your child?

_____

_____

_____

_____

_____

_____

_____

_____

_____

What have been your child's greatest successes?

1. _____

2. _____

3. _____

4. _____

5. _____

What are your hopes and wishes for your child in the years ahead?

_____

_____

_____

_____

_____

_____

_____

_____

_____

_____

_____

What are your child's dreams?

_____

_____

_____

_____

_____

What can you do to support those dreams?

_____

_____

_____

_____

_____

Chapter Fourteen
BONUS BABY: "SUPER DUKE"
"Professional Wrestlers, Super Heroes, and Gold's Gym"

After we adopted Hilary, Bob's law firm dissolved, which meant money was even tighter. Bob was working fourteen or fifteen hours a day, seven days a week. I missed a period, went for a pregnancy test, and you guessed it: I was pregnant.

With Jason, Spencer, Baby Hilly, and Tuan, my life was so chaotic that I had absolutely no idea when I got pregnant. I looked through my calendar but couldn't find any notes to help me. I couldn't even remember the dates of my latest period.

It was amazing how many stupid and idiotic things people said to me about my pregnancy. "You see," they would say knowingly, "once you adopted, you weren't nervous anymore, and that's why you got pregnant." I couldn't quite see the relationship between my emotional state and Bob's sperm, which were the problem. I just smiled and thanked them for their good wishes.

As my pregnancy progressed, the doctor and I estimated the due date as late December. She was planning a huge Christmas celebration at her house. Relatives were flying in from all over the country.

"You'd better not expect me to deliver this baby on Christmas Day," she said.

Nothing like a little pressure!

Luckily for my doctor and me, the baby — a boy — arrived at 1:30 a.m. on December 23. Bob said that since he was a Christmas Baby, he should be named Christopher. When Bob got back home after the delivery, he found all the kids up. The boys were taking care of Hilary and watching "Poltergeist" or some other horror movie. I went home at eight the next morning with our new baby. Hilary thought Christopher was a Cabbage Patch Doll.

From that day on, our house was pandemonium central. Going from "no children" to "one child" is like climbing up the side of a volcano that is about to erupt. Going from "one child" to "two children" is like teetering at the edge of the crater of the volcano after it has begun to spew ash into the atmosphere. Going from "two children to three children" hadn't been that big a change, but going from "three children to four children" tossed us right over the crater's rim into the molten lava.

At least, Jason and Spence were old enough to baby-sit and help out by coming up with the perfect nickname for the new baby. "We've got two for you to choose from," Jason told us. "It's either Twinkie or Duke." We chose Duke, which fit him to a tee.

Christopher loved costumes and make-believe. He had a Superman cape, which he called his "Superman cake," and he loved to run around the house, looking back over his shoulder to admire the way his cape flew out behind him. His nickname, "Duke," had already morphed into "Dukie" and during this period he became "Super Duke." Jason shortened that to "Supey," which eventually became "Soops."

Christopher also developed his own colorful language, as all young children do. He called the remote control the "mokey-troll," and The Three Stooges became the "Stoogins."

His most famous phrase was "No sank oo, scary dinosaur," which translates into English as "No thank you, scary dinosaur." This magical phrase evolved like this: Young Christopher was watching a TV show with his older brothers in which a scary dinosaur made an appearance. Christopher covered his eyes and said, "No sank oo, scary dinosaur," which apparently won him a reprieve from watching the program. In his wee brain he made the connection. If he didn't like what was happening, all he had to do was wave his arm, say these magic words, and the situation would instantly resolve itself in his favor.

I remember one time when my aunt was offering him some food to eat, which was not to his taste. He responded with a hearty "No sank oo scary dinosaur." She turned to me, and said, "He's so polite." In fact, "no sank oo, scary dinosaur" meant "get out of my face!" or "have you lost your mind?"

Still, Christopher's most profound toddler talent was sitting in his highchair, and EATING WHILE SLEEPING! With his eyes closed tight, he would scoop handful after handful of spaghetti from his bowl and stuff it into his mouth. He would slump lower and lower in his highchair, until his head was on the tray, but he would continue eating until we picked him up and put him into his crib.

Christopher also had a penchant for "taking off" or getting lost. Now, he never thought he was lost because he was Superman, and he always knew exactly where he was going. We went to a large Episcopal Church in Washington, DC, which Vice President George Bush and his wife Barbara also attended. One Easter, when Christopher was two and a half, he took off in the huge crowd. Bob and I were trying to find him, but it was impossible to see him.

Bob was calling "Christopher! Christopher! Has anyone seen a little boy in a sailor suit?"

"Yes!" the Vice President shouted back. "There he is," and much to the dismay of the Secret Service Agents, he began chasing after our son.

Christopher "ran away" many more times after that. Once he ran away at the beach in Seaside, Oregon where my "eccentric" Aunt Eldora found him on a street corner. Once, he left Sunday school and went to church by himself. Another time, he left Aunt Mabel's backyard and began wandering through her neighborhood.

After we moved from Washington, DC to Colorado, he graduated from "Superman" to Professional Wrestling. This phase lasted many, many years. He was also a Karate and Tae Kwon Do Champion, winning bronze and silver medals at the National Tournament, and he set swimming records in five events.

In middle school, he became a wonderful singer, and was known as "Elvis the Pelvis" after performing "Hardheaded Woman" in a school musical. He gave up swimming for acting and won two acting awards. His senior year in high school, he played Nathan Detroit in "Guys and Dolls." He lives in Southern California now where he attends college, works out at Gold's Gym, and is an actor.

He has a strong story that he tells himself: a story where his dreams come true.

Because he is our youngest child, Christopher hangs out with us more than the other children do. He's a great friend to everyone in the family and we know that he will be phenomenally successful at anything he undertakes.

~   ~   ~

When and where was your fourth child born?

_____

_____

_____

Write the story of your child's birth, giving as many details as possible:

_____

_____

_____

_____

_____

_____

_____

_____

_____

_____

_____

_____

_____

_____

_____

Write down your fourth child's first words:

_____

_____

_____

_____

_____

_____

Where and when did your fourth child walk?

_____

_____

_____

What are your five happiest memories of your child?

1. _____
2. _____
3. _____
4. _____
5. _____

What have been your child's greatest successes?

1. _____
2. _____

3. _____

4. _____

5. _____

Write three stories about your fourth child's infancy:

1. _____
_____
_____
_____
_____

2. _____
_____
_____
_____
_____

3. _____
_____
_____
_____
_____

Write three stories about his or her preschool years:

1. _____
_____
_____

2. _____

3. _____

Write three stories about your child's elementary school years (K-5th Grade):

1. _____

2. _____

3. _____

_____

_____

_____

Write three stories about your child's middle school years (6th, 7th, 8th Grade):

1. _____

_____

_____

_____

_____

2. _____

_____

_____

_____

_____

3. _____

_____

_____

_____

_____

Write three stories about your child's high school years:

1. _____

_____

_____

_____

_____

2. _____

_____

_____

_____

_____

3. _____

_____

_____

_____

_____

What are the stories that you tell yourself and others about your child?

_____

_____

_____

_____

_____

_____

_____

_____

_____

_____

_____

_____

_____

What are the "formative" stories you have told your child about him or herself?

_____

_____

_____

_____

_____

_____

_____

_____

_____

_____

_____

_____

_____

How do you think these stories have affected you?

_____

_____

_____

_____

_____

_____

_____

_____

How do you think these stories have affected your child?

_____

_____

_____

_____

_____

_____

_____

_____

What are your hopes and wishes for your child in the years ahead?

_____

_____

_____

_____

_____

What are your child's dreams?

_____

_____

_____

_____

_____

What can you do to support those dreams?

_____

_____

_____

_____

_____

⁓   ⁓   ⁓

If you have had more than four children, please use the notes pages in the back of the book to record additional stories

Chapter Fifteen
THERE'S LIFE AFTER CHILDREN!
or "Mommy's Doing What?"

Whew! I gave my children the best I had to give, and in the fall of Christopher's senior year of high school, I sat down and made a list of what was left undone on my "to do list." Writing books was at the top of the list. So that's what I've been doing.

Wherever you are in your life journey today — whether you're young and just starting out, or you've already built your career and family — it's never too early and never too late to begin writing your own story and living your passion. All you have to do is answer this simple question: What do I want? Once you've answered that question, all that remains is for you to commit fully to living the life you want.

Make a list of all the things you feel passionate about.

1. _____

2. _____

3. _____

4. _____

5. _____

6. _____
7. _____
8. _____
9. _____
10. _____

Make a list of your talents and skills.

1. _____
2. _____
3. _____
4. _____
5. _____
6. _____
7. _____
8. _____
9. _____
10. _____

Make a list of your successes in the past.

1. _____
2. _____
3. _____
4. _____
5. _____
6. _____
7. _____
8. _____

9. _____
10. _____

Make a list of the things that people have told you that you are good at.

1. _____
2. _____
3. _____
4. _____
5. _____
6. _____
7. _____
8. _____
9. _____
10. _____

Make a list of all the things you really care deeply about.

1. _____
2. _____
3. _____
4. _____
5. _____
6. _____
7. _____
8. _____
9. _____
10. _____

Now pick something on your list. Pick anything, and write a book about it! If you're reading this page, you've already accomplished more than most people ever do.

You've written your family's history. Congratulate yourself, and take the next step.

Write your book on your own, or join the Write Your Own Book Club, and I and the other members of the club will help you. I wish you every blessing on this wondrous journey we call life, and I encourage you to share your blessings with the world!

~　　　~　　　~

Additional Workbook Section

Divorce

Remarriage

Blended Families

Life Threatening Illness

Loss Of A Spouse

Loss Of A Child

Loss Of A Brother or Sister

Guide for writing your story:

- What happened? (Factual Chronology),
- How Did You Feel?
- What Did You Learn From The Experience?
- How Has It Changed You?
- How Does It Continue To Affect You In Negative And Positive Ways Today?
- What Would You Do Differently?
- What Helpful Advice Would You Give To Others In The Same Situation?

Divorce

Remarriage

Blended Families

_____

_____

_____

_____

_____

_____

_____

_____

_____

_____

_____

_____

_____

_____

_____

_____

_____

_____

_____

_____

_____

_____

_____

_____

_____

Life Threatening Illness

_____

_____

_____

_____

_____

_____

_____

_____

_____

_____

_____

_____

_____

_____

_____

_____

_____

_____

_____

_____

_____

_____

_____

Loss of A Spouse

_____

_____

_____

_____

_____

_____

_____

_____

_____

_____

_____

_____

_____

_____

_____

_____

_____

_____

_____

_____

_____

_____

_____

Loss of A Child

_____

_____

_____

_____

_____

_____

_____

_____

_____

_____

_____

_____

_____

_____

_____

_____

_____

_____

_____

_____

_____

_____

_____

_____

Loss of A Brother or Sister

_____

_____

_____

_____

_____

_____

_____

_____

_____

_____

_____

_____

_____

_____

_____

_____

_____

_____

_____

Notes

Notes

Notes

Notes

Notes

Notes

Bobbi's Bio

Bobbi McKenna is the author of "Telling Your Story." She's also the Founder and President of "The Write Your Own Book Club," which is dedicated to helping people become authors.

In addition to her writing and storytelling skills, Bobbi draws on her experiences working in government and politics for the U.S. Department of Defense; the U.S. Department of Education; the Office of the Mayor of New York City; the Capitol Hill Office of a Member of Congress in Washington, DC; and the Colorado State Office of a United States Senator.

In the nonprofit field, she was the Director of Management and Communications for the Alban Institute, headquartered on the grounds of the National Cathedral in Washington, DC. In that capacity, she designed and managed funding programs as well as systematized management systems. She also compiled and wrote "The Report on Vietnam Veteran's Memorials, Nationwide" for the Washington, DC-based Project for the Study of the Vietnam Generation.

Bobbi is an accomplished public speaker who has addressed the press at the National Press Club and has also received the Outstanding Briefer's award from the Defense Intelligence School.

Bobbi graduated from Chatham College in Pittsburgh, Pennsylvania, which she attended on a full scholarship, and did graduate work at George Washington University where she had two concurrent Teaching Fellowships and was a George Washington University Fellow.

She has lived in Portland, Oregon; Pittsburgh, Pennsylvania; Washington, DC; Charlottesville, Virginia; Taegu, Republic of Korea; Leavenworth, Kansas; New York City; Colorado; and California.

In her spare time, Bobbi is a professional singer who has performed with Leonard Bernstein and Robert Shaw at the Kennedy Center, Lincoln Center, and Carnegie Hall.

She has four children – three sons and a daughter adopted from Korea. She and her husband Robert have homes in Colorado and southern California.

Contact Bobbi at www.bobbimckenna.com.

Telling Your Story

Please send _____ copy/copies at $24.95 each plus handling and shipping. (see below)

For the quickest service go to www.bobbimckenna.com click on "Order Now", complete the online order form, and push "Submit!"

Ship to: _____

Name: _____

Address: _____

City: _____ State: _____ Zip: _____

Sales tax: 5.5% on products shipped to Colorado

U.S. Orders: $4.00 per book for handling and shipping.
International Orders: $9.00 per book for handling and shipping.
(Note: handling and shipping charges are based on actual cost and are subject to change.)

Payment: _____ Check or _____ Credit Card

_____ Visa _____ MasterCard _____ AMEX _____ Discover

Card Number: _____

Name on Card: _____

Expiration Date: _____

Address credit card bill is sent to: _____

City: _____ State: _____ Zip: _____

Telephone: _____

Email: _____

Postal Orders: Bobbi McKenna
                  7552 South Emerson Circle
                  Centennial, CO 80122

Please visit www.bobbimckenna.com to sign up for free newsletters, and to join The Write Your Own Book Club!